IENTS

"Susanne Sweeny has created an important and timely roadmap to successfully navigating life's complexities and stresses. Her book is a powerful guide to transcending the "tyranny of the urgent"; clarifying your life's mission, vision, and purpose; and taking control of your destiny. Its wisdom and practical advice will improve your sense of focus, your experience of living— and very likely your physical health as well. I recommend it highly!"

—Jeremy R. Geffen, MD, FACP
Medical oncologist and author of
The Journey Through Cancer:
Healing and Transforming the Whole Person

"Susanne Sweeny's book offers refreshing help on our journey of finding meaning, purpose, and legacy in our lives. A 'must read' for those wanting to make a difference in the frenetic 21st Century."

—Kenny Moore
HR Executive, former Catholic Monk, and
best-selling author of *The CEO and the Monk:*
One Company's Journey to Profit and Purpose.

"Got Stress? Here is a down-to-earth book that will not only help you survive today's pace but also bring joy back into your life. I recommend it to my corporate clients and to my friends!"

—Dr. Lucille Maddalena, Author and
Management Consultant

TRANSFORM STRESS INTO STRENGTH

To order additional copies of this title call:
1-877-421-READ (7323)
or please visit our Web site at
www.annotationbooks.com

If you enjoyed this quality custom-published book,
drop by our Web site for more books and information.

www.winepressgroup.com
"Your partner in custom publishing."

ISBN 13: 978-1-59977-010-9
ISBN 10: 1-59977-010-5
Library of Congress Catalog Card Number: 2007929102

CONTENTS

Section IV Getting Control of Your Time
Beyond the "Tyranny of the Urgent"

PREFACE

F or years I was riddled with stress and anxiety. I read every book and article on the subject, trying to get control of my hectic life. Unfortunately, most of what I found were temporary "quick fixes" for stress: breathe deeply, exercise more, *stop worrying!* I sensed there was something deeper I needed to understand and work on, but I didn't have a clue what it was, nor did I know how to go about addressing it.

I should mention that this search for a solution to stress took place somewhere over two decades of a career working for the IBM Corporation. At one point I was managing four hundred people while simultaneously raising a blended and extended family—all predictable sources of stress. Before managing this large group, I was designing and conducting IBM leadership development classes on teamwork, conflict resolution, enhancing personal effectiveness, and stress management! In designing the workshops, I used a variety of well-proven, personal assessment tools and experiential learning to help guide individuals through the difficult process of introspection and reinvention of themselves, seeking a transformation "from stress to strength."

Of course, in the business world the focus on personal effectiveness is aimed at helping employees and the company to become more productive. I later extended my teaching beyond IBM to other firms, big and small, for-profit and nonprofit, government and private sector—from school systems, to the military, to ballet companies. I was amazed at the response to the material presented. The concepts seemed to apply everywhere!

After leaving the corporate world to become a counselor, life coach, and seminar leader, I realized that the concepts and tools I'd been using to train groups in interpersonal communication were just as useful to people in their personal lives. Perhaps they were even *more* useful here, with the end goal being a life of greater satisfaction and fulfillment. What I discovered through a series of case studies, research work, student feedback, and graduate school study was that *stress is just an external symptom of a life that's perceived to be out of control and out of adjustment.* Like a car whose wheels are out of alignment, the entire vehicle can't perform well until it's rebalanced.

Personal dissatisfaction and discontent, I discovered, are related to a person's perceived purpose in life, mental state, and ongoing allocation of his or her time. When people believe they can't control events, they become increasingly overwhelmed and stressed out by them. So, gaining some sense of control over our life, our mind, and our time combines to bring balance and order to the chaotic stream of input we may be fielding from the world around us. Yet dealing with only *one* of these key components will fail to achieve a comprehensive and permanent solution to our discontent. We must stop, address, and "tune" all of them.

What amazes me is how current this topic remains. In November, 2007, Dr. Mehmet Oz, vice chairman of surgery at New York Presbyterian/Columbia University and coauthor of his latest book, *You . . . Staying Young,* was on the *Oprah Winfrey Show,* speaking as an expert on health. Oprah asked him, "What is the number one *major ager* today?" Without hesitation he said, *"Unequivocally, it's Stress!!* And it's much worse now than five years ago!" Then he went on to touch on some of the concepts in this book, like the mind/body connection and the power of prayer and meditation.

At the end of every workshop I gave on this topic, someone would invariably ask, "So, where is your book?" They wanted to have the material and assessments packaged in a way that they could easily use and reuse them at home for themselves, their partners, friends, and family members. I understood that need for constant reinforcement . . . because every time I conducted the workshop I felt re-energized myself, and it reinforced the changes I had made in my own life.

PERSONAL TRANSFORMATION

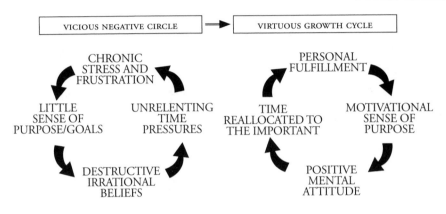

| VICIOUS NEGATIVE CIRCLE | → | VIRTUOUS GROWTH CYCLE |

Figure 1

So, what is my approach? Many of us face a common dilemma in life: *a vicious circle* running in reverse. We rarely take the time or have the *know-how* to examine our lives deeply; most of us are just not introspective enough to do so. In addition, we may lack the clarity of well-grounded values, a mission, a vision, and clear goals. Then, too, we impose on ourselves unrelenting time pressures and inappropriate and destructive emotional responses to half-understood stimuli. These factors all reinforce each other in negative ways, resulting in increasing levels of stress and frustration within. *How can it be different?*

By intervening to analyze your life, create your life plan, reallocate your time, and redefine your responses to everyday events, you can reverse the negative, "vicious circle" and replace it with a *virtuous growth cycle,* one that continuously builds personal strength. The ultimate, achievable goal is a life of harmony, fulfillment, contentment, and inner joy. And, most importantly, it's about a life of balance and congruence—the alignment of your actions and use of your time with your true personal values and life purpose.

The workshop this book mirrors was experiential in nature, and so is this book. On your journey *from stress to strength* you will be taking several personal assessments, developing a mission and vision statement, analyzing seven key areas of your life, and filling in a time management matrix. So, I strongly suggest you have a personal journal or notebook at hand to record emerging insights as you read. You also may want to copy the assessment materials *first* so that you can share them with a fellow traveler down the road in time.

Yours for motivation and transformation,
Susanne Sweeny

ACKNOWLEDGMENTS

There are many people who have contributed to this book either through their encouragement or their ideas, or by being role models of personal strength. One stands well above the others. He's been my emotional support when I'm frazzled, my critic when needed, my guide when I seemed lost, and my editor from beginning to end. That person is my husband, Doug. His patience and steadfastness had a truly calming effect on me.

Finally, I need to acknowledge that it is the Spirit of God within me who gives me the strength, insight, and perseverance to prevail through all the challenges in my life, including the writing of this book.

SECTION I

"All Stressed Up and No Place to Go"

An Inside View of You

CHAPTER ONE

LOSING YOUR SONG

"A caged bird sings with a fearful trill of things
unknown, but longed for still."
—Maya Angelou

When I was a little girl I had a beautiful and happy little canary that used to sing all day long. His name was *Dickie Bird.* One day my mom was cleaning out his cage with a small vacuum cleaner attachment when the phone rang. As she stretched out to answer the telephone and simultaneously leaned down to turn off the vacuum cleaner, her other arm tilted up and she accidentally sucked poor little Dickie Bird into the vacuum cleaner hose! As you can imagine, she was frantic about what had happened to my poor canary, so she dropped the phone, ripped open the vacuum cleaner bag, and discovered there, amidst the dirt and debris, a bird-shaped dust ball with big eyes that was my darling little bird, completely in shock. She picked him up, rushed him into the bathroom, threw him into the sink, and drenched him with torrents of ice-cold water!

Seeing him trembling and shaking with his big, wide, terrified eyes, she grabbed the hair dryer, put it on high, and blew him dry with hurricane-force winds! Believe it or not, Dickie Bird survived that traumatic episode . . . but he never did sing again.

Like that little bird, many of us have *lost our song,* and for the same reason. The stress we've been through and still have in our lives has robbed us of our joy. Often in my life I've felt just like my bird probably felt that day. I'm just sitting in my cage at home or at work, singing away, and, all of a sudden, I'm sucked up, wrung out, and blown away by a set of powerful forces way beyond *my* control. Has that ever happened to you? I think life does it to all of us at some point. Sometimes it's a single, powerful blow that knocks us off our perch, and at other times it's just one little incident after another, until all of a sudden we realize we've had one–too–many blows or incidents—and we just fall apart.

Sometimes, like Dickie Bird, we are never the same again after a trauma. Oh sure, we live through it, but it takes its toll on our minds and our bodies . . . and we just can't sing anymore. However, sometimes what doesn't kill us makes us stronger, and after we have gone through the storm and survived it, we have a *different* song to sing, and maybe even a *sweeter* one that can help other people with their life traumas.

Some of you reading this may, at this moment, be enduring a life filled with stress. My life was, and is, filled with incredible stress, and yet somehow I am surviving—and, at times, actually thriving. I want to share with you two different circumstances and types of stress from my life: one a single, uncontrollable traumatic incident; the other, the cumulative affect of many stress-producing factors, some of them the result of my own decisions. There were valuable insights I gained from each.

Trauma and Stress

The date was July 7, 1977, and my oldest son, Michael, was seven-years-old. We lived on a safe, quiet cul-de-sac where he and his brother, Jeffrey, and other neighborhood children were, one afternoon, happily playing in a huge pile of sand left by a landscaper. Within less than a minute our lives changed in dramatic fashion. A teenager on a motorcycle came barreling through the cul-de-sac, lost control, and ran into the pile of sand. Michael tried to push his brother out of the way of the oncoming motorbike and, in the process, got hit in the head by the heavy, speeding cycle. The details of those hours, days, and weeks are now blurry, and yet the feelings are so clear thirty years later that I can still relive them as if the event were yesterday. I can still see the fear in my little boy's eyes as he tried to be strong after the accident.

At the hospital, they called in a brain surgeon and a plastic surgeon, who cautiously explained to me that they had to open his skull from ear to ear and take out the bone fragments, as well as a piece of his brain. They informed me of three ways this might turn out. He could die or be paralyzed or, hopefully, the surgery could go well, but he would, in any case, have a long recuperation period, wearing a helmet every day to protect the brain where the skull had been. Then, in six months, they would operate again to put a plate in his head, and then the plastic surgeon would take muscle from his leg to cover the plate.

Those eight hours of waiting for that first surgery to be over were probably the longest and most stressful in my life. As I sat waiting, worrying, and praying, a flood of thoughts came to mind. When Michael was just fourteen months old he'd had an emergency tonsillectomy. He had a fever of 106 degrees, and they first had to bring that down before they operated. Because he was so young, they didn't want to give him anesthesia until right before surgery. So, he was awake when they took him away from me. He held out his little hand crying, "Mommy," and I remember thinking how awful it was that this had to happen to him at such a young age. Little did I know what was still in store for this child!

I reflected on the moment, a week before the accident, that Michael had come to me asking if he could ride his bicycle to town, a mile down the street, with all his friends. I said, "Absolutely not. It's too dangerous." He cried and said, "But everyone else's parents said it was OK." I blurted out something that my mom had always said in situations like this: "Better *you* should cry now than *I* should cry later." Well, ironically, here we were in brain surgery—and all his friends riding their bikes to town were just fine. And was *I* crying!

I also remembered that before the accident, on the morning of July 7, 1977, I had been sobbing over something so trivial that I couldn't even remember what it was that had made me cry. After a couple of days living at the hospital, my husband and I went out to a fast food place to try and eat, although we didn't really feel like eating. I couldn't eat, sleep, or focus on anything else in life. I watched everyone coming and going. Their lives were still the same, whereas *ours* had forever changed. As many of you can testify, once something *really bad* happens to you, it makes you realize how vulnerable you truly are and how easily something life-changing could happen to you again.

Thank God, the surgery was successful! We all got through the next six months, while waiting for the second surgery. Of course, it was difficult for Michael to enter the third grade with a helmet on his head. Kids made fun of him. He wasn't allowed to do sports, and he developed a speech impediment that was very frustrating for him. His brother, Jeff, an adorable, outgoing, lovable, and fun little boy seemed to be OK at first, but over time we realized the effect the accident had had on him, as well. Perhaps he felt guilty because his brother had pushed *him* out of the way of the oncoming motorcycle. In any case, the incredible amount of attention his brother was getting led Jeff to act out in other ways to get our attention. For the rest of Michael's childhood, Michael did everything he could *not* to get any attention.

But the saga and stress continued. The surgeon sat us down before the second surgery to tell us that *bone fragments* had inadvertently been left in the brain during the emergency surgery. He told us that if they went in deep enough to try to remove them, Michael could be blinded or paralyzed, but if they left them in, they could get infected at any time. An infection could be a very serious thing, and if we chose that option, we had to watch him all the time . . . and *every* time he had a fever he would have to be checked out by a physician—and this was a kid who ran high fevers often. Obviously, the older he became without an infection developing, the better his chances. *What a decision to make!*

"How can I make this decision?" I asked the doctor. "If it were your child, what would you do?" After much thought, he said he would probably leave the bone fragments alone. So that is what we did. And, as you can imagine, through the years we watched and worried, and the more we watched and worried, the less Michael told us about the times when he got hurt or felt feverish.

This was a single, traumatic event that affected our entire family forever. We can't possibly look back and determine that if this hadn't happened, our lives would have been better. I know my faith and personal relationship with God, along with the support of my mother and some close friends, helped get me through it. In the Bible it says that God's number of completion and perfection is *seven,* so I believed that because of this accident happening on July 7, 1977 and Mike being seven-years-old on that day, that maybe God was doing a "good work" of some kind in him. I knew He had many other plans in mind for Michael's future, so perhaps this was the needed preparation for them.

One example of God's unique and special plans for Michael happened when, after college, he decided to volunteer for the Peace Corps and spent more than two years in Guatemala helping families in a very poor village. Over the years he has had three other exceptionally traumatic events in his life. There's no question in my mind that this trauma in his early life made him exceptionally strong within and a much more compassionate person altogether.

In many ways this demanding experience with my son was the beginning of my journey toward understanding stress. Until this episode, I was fun-loving and easygoing, and I felt the invulnerability of youth. But after Michael's accident my mind-set changed, and I became more cautious, more reactive, and, sad to say, *a worrier.* One of my initial insights from this experience was that stress, while it may start from a single incident, can become a chronic, long-term syndrome in us. It was also clear to me now that stress affects us both *mentally* and *physically.* Like a virus, it could spread through the family, it seemed, but it affected each of us differently and in unpredictable ways.

I learned that stress is *relative.* Being caught in a traffic jam and missing an important appointment can seem unbearably stressful at the time, until you get a call that something much worse has happened. As much as I hated it, too, I could see that going through a serious life-stressor, such as our family had, could make each of us stronger, if we kept the goal foremost to *turn our stress into strength!*

The *Last Straw* and Stress

Sometimes there's no single, cataclysmic event that creates stress, but a cumulative series of factors that, added together, can send us over the edge. Between the ages of thirty-five and fifty-five, I was divorced, raised two boys, eventually remarried, and took on two more children, which gave me four teenagers, all between the ages of twelve and fourteen, plus two dogs and a cat! (No *Dickie Bird!*) The stress of that sudden houseful was compounded by a very complicated set of ex-spouse issues. But I had even more on my plate than the exhausting roles of mother and stepmom.

I worked at a major corporation, commuted two hours daily, and was responsible for managing hundreds of employees. During this same timeframe, I cared for my elderly parents;

one with a broken hip that never healed (Dad) and the other with Alzheimer's disease (Mom). There was no sibling to help me with this since I'm an only child.

A typical weekend began with a two-hour drive two states away to visit my parents and take them to doctor's appointments and to arrange and *rearrange* their home health care since it never seemed to work out. I would sit in the back seat of the car writing performance appraisals on the ride down as my husband drove. He would fix whatever was wrong with my parents' house while I fixed their caregiver schedule and took them out for walks or dinner. Then we rushed back home the next day to catch up on all the kids' activities and to find out what they were doing that they shouldn't have been. Then I'd do the week's food shopping (three carts' worth), laundry, and housecleaning.

My husband would help the kids with their homework while I worked on my own. (I was getting my masters degree in counseling and education.) We would drop into bed each night exhausted. My husband would go directly to sleep, while I woke up every hour with hot flashes. Monday morning, everyone else arrived at work refreshed, but not me!

Of course, while working with my parents' health issues I had several of my own: two major surgeries and a couple of minor ones. I also have a syndrome called fibromyalgia, which, incidentally, is caused by stress. One year I was actually excited about having a hysterectomy, because I knew the surgery would force me to rest for a few weeks. Trying to juggle all of this taught me that many small stressors can add up to a *huge* stress. I learned that some stress can be self-imposed as we make decisions every day that add to our stress load. For example: we take that job promotion, attend graduate school, or try to be the best stepmom ever. Secondly, I learned that *cumulative stress* can be just as devastating and unhealthy as *traumatic incident* stress. And finally, I learned that stress can come from many different sources (i.e., career, finances, relationships, health, etc.) and be compounded by their combinations.

In the middle of those very stressful years, I decided to read up on stress and see what I could do personally to relieve it and survive it! Since everyone I knew seemed to have some of the same issues, I created a "stress management" workshop to share what I learned and what was working for me (initially putting extra stress on myself). I began conducting seminars in my company (IBM) and then in other corporations nearby. Many firms encouraged this, because stress was known to have a major impact on productivity, absenteeism, and health insurance expense. And for me, teaching was good personal therapy. I noticed that every time I gave this workshop, I always felt better. I could put events into better perspective and regain a sense of control over my life.

Understanding Stress

So, what exactly *is* stress, anyway? Every day we read headlines like these:

"We're sick of being stressed out."

"Our lives are all crumpled up with stress."

"We have a belly full of toxic stress."

And just as we're getting more stressed out reading about stress, we read:

"Job stress can be satisfying."

"Stress hormones aid in remembering."

"Surprise: Stress is good."

So, which is it? Is stress a *good* thing or a *bad* thing? Which of the headlines holds true? The answer: *All of them!*

Stress, in itself, is neither good, nor bad. It's really just the sum of the physical and mental responses each of us has to life's everyday events. What typically happens is that when something unexpected happens to us, whether we have just run out of gas or had a family member die, we automatically evaluate the situation mentally. We decide *instantly* if it's threatening, how we can deal with it, and if we have the ability to do so. If the demands of a situation seem overwhelming and feel beyond our ability to handle, we label the situation "stressful" and demonstrate some of those classic stress responses: fight or flight. But *our thoughts* are the critical factor. And since no two people are alike, and we all have different coping skills, then no two people handle stress in exactly the same way.

What Is Stress?

But we're getting ahead of ourselves. What is stress, anyway, and who discovered it? One could argue that since techniques to relieve stress, like meditation, were developed five thousand years ago by ancient Indian spiritual seers, they must certainly have had the concept of stress in mind before trying to resolve it. But, dialing forward to more modern times, the contemporary founder of the "Science of Stress" was a European doctor, Hans Selye.

Back in the 1930s it was gradually understood that the concepts of anxiety, frustration, distress, despair, fear, and exhaustion were somehow related and could all be collected into a broad category. It was Selye who first formalized these notions, borrowing an English word from physics, "stress," to label the body's nonspecific response to any demand made on it. It was a good analogy, and the term stuck. Like an overloaded bridge or a metal cable pulled too tightly, as human beings we feel muscular tension and often feel we could *snap* if it gets any worse.

One of Selye's most notable contributions was the idea that stress could be either *positive* or *negative,* just like radiation can be a positive cure or a health risk if you're exposed to it. He labeled the two types of stress as *eustress* and *distress.* "Eu" is a prefix meaning "good or well," and, of course, "dis" is a prefix meaning to "deprive, fail, or cease."

Eustress is the positive type of stress. It's the feeling you get when you are about to kiss someone new and exciting for the first time . . . or when riding the rapids . . . or getting ready for a much-needed vacation . . . or before the birth of a long-wanted child. It's the adrenalin rush you get before giving a well-rehearsed speech or stepping up to bat, when you know you're pretty good and you're enjoying the moment. In nature, the pearl is formed by the stress of a sand particle against the skin of an oyster, and the diamond is pressed into being by the stress on subterranean levels of coal.

Distress, on the other hand, is a negative stress. We all have lots of examples of distress, and it's usually the type of stress we think of first. It may be the conflict and guilt you feel when you have a deadline at work and your child is expecting you to be at his or her little league game. You feel over your head at work, and your boss expects too much; you are sure your next performance rating will be bad. Your son is failing in school, and your daughter is running around with the wrong crowd. You are an only child taking care of a sick parent. Your spouse is going through a midlife crisis and expects you to handle everything. You are overwhelmed to the point of breaking.

Another way of describing stress is to think about the physiological "fight or flight syndrome." When confronted with stress, man tends either to *fight back* or to *flee.* Whether it's a tiger or your mother-in-law, you have a tendency to do one or the other. Why? Stress is really a biochemical reaction. It is the *fight or flight* adrenal rush that readies a body for short-term challenges, such as when a tired pilot must make an emergency landing. The adrenal gland releases cortisol, a hormone which, in the short term, increases the ability of immune cells to kill damaged or infected cells. It "pushes them to their greatest capacity to perform." The stress response is natural and essential to survival. Yet, of course, sometimes the expectation of an event is more stressful than the actual event itself.

> Sometimes the expectation of an event is more stressful than the actual event itself.

OPTIMAL STRESS

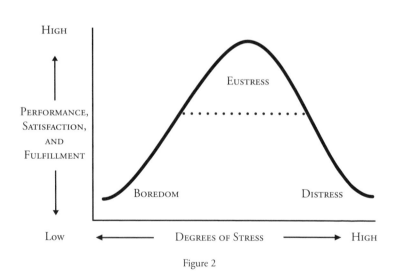

Figure 2

The eustress curve diagram illustrates the concept that for any performance-related activity there is an optimal amount of stress. If you are giving a speech, stress will help you prepare, think quickly, and express your thoughts clearly, in ways that will benefit listeners. Too little stress leads to a very boring life, and too much stress can make you sick, so the *optimal* satisfaction level is in the middle. Like the strings of a violin, when pulled too tightly they will screech, too loosely they won't play, but pulled *just right* they will make beautiful music. Eustress keeps us motivated and causes us to stretch ourselves toward peak performance.

So it seems that the core issue is not how do we eliminate all stress, but how do we maintain our daily stress at an optimal level so that we can experience peak performance in our goal-seeking? This issue is never resolved, because our stress level is always changing. The Chinese word for stress, however, combines two ancient symbols—one for *danger,* and one for *opportunity.* Indeed, stress can be a friend or a foe, depending on whether we use it well or poorly.

Webster's definition of stress relates it to other terms used in physics: "pressure, strain, or a factor that induces bodily or mental tension." Stress can involve anything that changes your comfortable style of living or pushes you beyond a "comfort zone."

A Comprehensive and Personal Approach

There are many books, courses, and TV shows on the individual topics of stress management, time management, life management, and even *mind management.* In the pages that follow I would like to take you on a personal journey that explores all of these subjects in a comprehensive and holistic way. In these pages you will learn to:

1. Identify symptoms of your stress.

2. Establish your life's purpose.

3. Explore mental traps that keep you from progress on the "seven key life dimensions."

4. Discover how to find time to bring change to your life.

We will begin this journey by guiding you to become more introspective about your life, using a series of easy–to–take questionnaires and self-assessment tools. These will highlight the immediate issues confronting you on a daily basis: symptoms of discomfort, anxiety, frustration, and other daily stressors that signal *all is not well.* We will then examine your tolerance for stress and your personality type. In Chapter Three, we will go deeper, looking through the lens of the "seven key dimensions of life" so that you can better understand your *personal stress profile.*

During the course of our journey we will define a *personal fulfillment gap,* the difference between where you want to be in each key dimension and where you are right now. That done, we'll provide you with tools to develop a focused *action plan* designed specifically to close those gaps. By book's end, you will have a much deeper understanding of the personal factors impacting your long-term fulfillment and happiness and a practical approach for addressing them.

CHAPTER TWO

STARVE YOUR STRESS. FEED YOUR JOY

"Stress: The confusion created when one's mind overrides the body's basic desire to choke the living daylights out of some jerk that desperately deserves it."

—Anonymous

B efore we begin to assess your personal sources of stress, there's one more important concept to understand. It's the mind-body connection and the three barometers of stress with regard to it: physiological, emotional, and behavioral. They will be different for each individual. Some examples of stress symptoms by category are:

- ◆ **Physiological:** butterflies in the stomach, dry mouth, sweating, yawning, face flushed, palms wet, rapid heart, change in appetite.

- ◆ **Emotional:** fear, resentment, hostility, bitterness, anxiety, loneliness, frustration, guilt, bad temper, confusion.

- ◆ **Behavioral:** procrastination, lethargy, inability to concentrate, aggression, withdrawal, impotence, trouble sleeping, drug/alcohol abuse.

You may now be thinking, *Yes, I know all that, and I have many of those symptoms, but how does my body know the difference between the good (eustress) and the bad (distress)?* Our bodies and minds are so strongly linked together that the body, by design, intuitively knows the difference.

Stress is essential to active living. In fact, life *without* stress would be a little bit like having a brand new Porsche and driving it only in the driveway. *Why?* Because we would be doing much less with our new car than the vehicle was capable of doing. For human beings, life without stress would be similarly less challenging, and less fulfilling.

What brings us happiness is meeting life's obstacles and overcoming them. But damage occurs when stress levels remain at a constant high over long periods of time. A recent study showed it took nine days longer for the overstressed caregiver of a chronically ill family member to heal from wounds than it took other persons of the same age. And because the world is relentless in doling out stress, it's easier to be *ready for it* than to try to control all those random forces coming at you daily. It's not stress that's the problem; it's insufficient recovery periods. Battle-weary soldiers get "R and R." Many of us in "the battle of life" need it, as well.

Why do we even *care* about stress if it's a natural and essential element of life? Because *distress* can kill us! Stress can cause coronary disease, ulcers, headaches, hypertension, viral infections, asthma attacks, elevated heart rates, backaches, ulcers, mental depression, short tempers, crying jags, insomnia, fibromyalgia—and even cancer.

"How many of you, in your heart of hearts, believe that stress can make you sick?" Esther Steinberg, a leading researcher on the link between the brain and the immune system, knew it was a loaded question to ask an audience packed with scientists. She asked it anyway . . . at a meeting of the American Association for the Advancement of Science. Everyone's hand shot up without hesitation. Five years prior, she had asked the same question, and only a few doctors had raised their hands.

In her book, *The Balance Within: The Science Connecting Health and Emotions,* Steinberg tells why scientists today are changing their minds. Without getting too technical (because then even *I* wouldn't understand), animal experiments suggest ties between illness and brain hormones released during periods of stress. Some of these findings have pointed the way to discoveries about human stress. People who react to stress with a lower–than–normal release of stress hormones are particularly vulnerable to inflammatory ailments such as asthma, rheumatoid arthritis, fibromyalgia, skin allergies, and many more ailments. Studies show that in these cases higher levels of stress hormones help to protect against those diseases. Scientists are exploring the possibility of developing drugs that might gear up the stress response enough to combat the illnesses.

At the other end of the spectrum, prolonged stress that triggers a chronic overload of stress hormones, such as the release of cortisol, impairs the body's ability to fight infectious disease. Sheldon Cohen, a psychologist at Carnegie Mellon University in Pittsburgh, is known for injecting cold viruses into healthy volunteers. He consistently finds that those who report being under the greatest amount of stress develop the worst colds. And Ohio State University psychologist Janice Kierolt-Glaser has produced research that strongly ties stress-hormone surges in quarreling spouses to physical illness.

As previously mentioned, Dr. Mehmet Oz appeared on the *Oprah Winfrey Show* in late 2007 as part of his regular health update, discussing his new book, *Staying Young*. When Oprah asked him directly what the number one *major ager* is today, his answer was, "unequivocally it's *Stress!*" Stress cuts oxygen flow to the heart and the brain and also alters immune function, Dr. Oz said. He went on to explain that the pituitary gland and hypothalamus are the physiological sites of the mind/body connection. When these two organs are stimulated by stress, the adrenal gland turns on, releasing chemicals to catapult the body into the primal *flight or fight* response.

The Vegus nerve originates in the brain and is the counteracting force that calms the body down. The Vegus nerve ("vegus" means *wandering*) has branches that go to the heart, lungs, and intestinal tract, and three-fourths of what it does is to send information back to your brain for immediate use. When there is too much content, the brain short circuits. So how do we tap into the Vegus nerve? Dr. Oz says *meditating* and *praying* are high on the list of ways to connect to it.

Mind and Body: What's the Connection?

The link between mental and physical wellbeing was discovered at least 2,300 years ago, when the philosopher Plato said that we cannot separate the soul from the body, that we must understand the *whole person*. Science has now confirmed it: Stress cuts oxygen flow to the heart and the brain and also alters the functioning of the immune system. The mind and body are more than married; they are intimately united. When one suffers, the other *sympathizes*. That's why, when we are feeling sick for a long period of time, it starts to affect us mentally—and why when we are going through a very stressful time in our personal life or work situation, we begin to get physically sick. So, how big a problem is this?

Here's a quick quiz:

According to the American Medical Association (AMA), what percentage of illness is stress-related?

A. 59%

B. 67%

C. 80%

You guessed it; the answer is 80 percent! At least 800,000 people miss work each day, which costs businesses $150 billion a year . . . and another $100 to $200 billion per year in productivity and medical expenses. It's certainly a major issue for women. In fact, 250,000 women participated in a write-in poll conducted by the U.S. Department of Labor Women's Bureau approximately twenty years ago. This is believed to be the largest response to a poll of working women ever received, tallied, and evaluated. Respondents were asked what they considered to be their biggest problem at work. The number one response was "too much stress." Respondents felt rushed and stated they never had enough time to get the job done (62 percent). The number two response was not getting paid what the job was worth (49 percent), and the third issue was the need for better benefits (44 percent).

A similar study done by the Daytimers® Corporation of 1300 workers, both men and women, found that 62 percent (the exact same percentage) believed that their number one problem at work was stress! However, we have said that *some stress* is good and drives us to excel. So, is there an optimal amount of stress we should have in our life to keep us motivated but not get us down and depleted? The answer, of course, is *yes*, and each of us needs to find the perfect balance of stimulus and stress that works best for us.

One of the most recent studies published in the *Journal of the American Medical Association* in late 2007 found "very solid scientific evidence" that job stress contributes to coronary trouble. Based on a study of 972 men and women, the AMA found that chronic on-the-job stress *doubles* the risk that someone who has had one heart attack will have another. And, according to this latest research, conducted by Dr. Corine Aboa-Eboule at the Universite Laval in Quebec, stress contributes susceptibility not only to cardiovascular disease but also to depression and HIV/AIDS, as well.

Sources of Stress

So now we know a little about stress, its positive and negative aspects and its physical and mental dimensions. What do you think is the number one cause of anxiety for the average citizen? Believe it or not, according to well-publicized research from the Dale Carnegie Institute, for 41 percent of people, *speaking in public* is the highest stress-inducer. *Fear of dying* was reported in seventh place on the "sources of stress" list in this study, with 19 percent of respondents reporting it as their highest stressor.

Isn't it interesting that both sexes fear speaking in public over dying?! Does that make sense? It means that people at a funeral would rather be in the casket than giving the eulogy. I guess if they were dead they wouldn't be getting any negative audience feedback. Actually, that might not be true; they could be getting their "final feedback!"

Here's another quick quiz:

According to a 2000 Harvard University study, compared to twenty years ago, the average employed worker in the U.S.A. is working about:

A. A month less

B. The same

C. A month more

The answer is "C." In fact, the precise number is 163 hours *more* per year! Also, workers are taking 15 percent less vacation time. In fact, 28 percent of American workers didn't take any vacation days at all in the past year. What happened to the "great strides we're making toward working shorter hours" in order to be able to spend more leisure time with family? What happened to Alvin Toffler's *electronic cottages* where, aided by our terrific technology, we could work from home and get everything done more quickly? (And Toffler wrote about that long before there was an Internet, cell phones, or Blackberry® PDAs!)

Since commuting to work can be so stressful, it's good news that more people are now able to work from home, but they are having trouble (stress) transitioning from working at an office to working in their homes. More and more employees report they are now "always connected" to work, 24/7, through all this new technology . . . so much so they can't distinguish between work and family/home. The boundaries have become blurred.

Stress Is Up . . . *Everywhere!*

One of the most recent and comprehensive studies of stress was conducted by Harris Interactive, for the American Psychology Association. Their survey of 1,848 adults in September 2007 found that 32 percent of Americans report experiencing extreme levels of stress on a regular basis. Money and work are the biggest causes of stress (73 percent and 74 percent respectively), up from just 59 percent just one year earlier.

The pressure is really getting to us, as nearly half (48 percent) of respondents said their stress had increased in the last five years. Other key findings include:

- 82 percent of women, versus 72 percent of men, said they had experienced a physical symptom of stress within the past month, such as sleep problems, overeating, skipping meals, or using prescription drugs.

- 48 percent of single people said stress had hurt their social lives, versus 34 percent of married couples and 38 percent of divorced persons.

- 52 percent of employees said they had considered or made a career change based on workplace stress. Leading sources of stress at work included low salaries, heavy workload, long hours, and lack of advancement opportunities.

- 54 percent reported arguing or fighting with a family member in the past month—a spouse (32 percent), children (15 percent), or parents (12 percent).

- Lower income workers (households under $50,000) reported feeling more stress *physically* (80 percent) than higher income employees (74 percent) and *psychologically* (77 percent, versus 68 percent). And they had more irritability (54 percent, versus 46 percent) and lack of energy and motivation (51 percent, versus 40 percent).

One conclusion of the researchers: America is becoming a nation of *multitaskers* as people's lives become increasingly more complicated. And unfortunately, there seems to be less time than ever to recharge our internal batteries.

Our decision to stay busy at all hours and attempt to do *five things at once* just isn't working! In the November, 2007, issue of *The Atlantic Monthly,* a key study by Walter Kirn states that multitasking messes with our brains in several ways. Multitasking requires a complex mental balancing act, one where we're constantly switching among different regions of the brain that specialize in visual processing and physical coordination. Simultaneously, it appears to shortchange some of the higher brain activities related to memory and learning. We concentrate on *the act of concentration* at the expense of whatever it is we're supposed to be concentrating on. Even worse, studies find that multitasking boosts the level of stress-related hormones, such as cortisol and adrenaline, and wears our systems down through biochemical friction, prematurely aging us.

> Thirty-two percent of Americans report experiencing extreme levels of stress on a regular basis.

In the short term, the confusion, fatigue, and chaos created by multitasking hamper our ability to focus and analyze; and, in the long term, they may cause it to atrophy. The irony of multitasking is that it's overall goal, to get more done in less time, turns out to be an illusion. In fact, it actually *slows* our thinking and dumbs us down. It forces us to chop competing tasks into pieces, set them aside, then hunt for the pile we're interested in, pick up its pieces, review the rules for putting the pieces back together, then attempt to do so. A brain performing two tasks simultaneously will, because of all this back and forth stress, flail away in a frenzied state and eventually becomes fatigued. Novelist Walter Kirn says this approach to work becomes frenetic, "like running up and down a beach repairing a row of sand castles as the tide comes in." This seems an apt metaphor for the frustration, stress, and ineffectiveness we know so well.

Assessing Your Personal Stressors

Knowing what causes stress *in general* is interesting, but what about *your* stress, specifically? In the next few pages we will introduce some personalized assessments so you can better understand the stress in your life and how it may be affecting you. If we avoid, as much as possible, those factors that contribute to our stress and, at the same time, spend more time and energy in areas that give us joy, our life will begin to turn around. We will starve our stress and feed our joy.

The first tool was created by Doctors Thomas H. Holmes and Richard H. Rahe, developed at the University of Washington Medical School. It's a widely-used scale for measuring stress in terms of 43 life events. As noted, some stress is necessary to provide a challenging and fulfilling life, but too much stress is harmful. The developers of this inventory say a person scoring less than 150 on their scale has only a 37 percent chance of becoming seriously ill during the next two years. A score of 150 to 300 raises the odds of illness to 51 percent, and a 300 plus score means you have an 80 percent chance of becoming ill. To find *your* score, check the events that occurred in your life during the past two years. Then, add up the total values. When you're done, continue reading and learn more.

How's Your Stress Score?

Rank	Event	Value	Your Score
1.	DEATH OF SPOUSE	100	_____
2.	DIVORCE	73	_____
3.	MARITAL SEPARATION	65	_____
4.	JAIL TERM	63	_____
5.	DEATH OF CLOSE FAMILY MEMBER	63	_____
6.	PERSONAL INJURY OR ILLNESS	63	_____
7.	MARRIAGE	60	_____
8.	FIRED FROM WORK	47	_____
9.	MARITAL RECONCILIATION	45	_____
10.	RETIREMENT	45	_____
11.	CHANGE IN FAMILY MEMBER'S HEALTH	44	_____
12.	PREGNANCY	40	_____
13.	SEX DIFFICULTIES	39	_____
14.	ADDITION TO FAMILY	39	_____
15.	BUSINESS READJUSTMENT	39	_____
16.	CHANGE IN FINANCIAL STATUS	38	_____
17.	DEATH OF CLOSE FRIEND	37	_____
18.	CHANGE TO DIFFERENT LINE OF WORK	36	_____
19.	CHANGE IN NUMBER OF MARITAL ARGUMENTS	35	_____
20.	MORTGAGE OR LOAN OVER $50,000	31	_____
21.	FORECLOSURE OF MORTGAGE OR LOAN	30	_____
22.	CHANGE IN WORK RESPONSIBILITIES	29	_____
23.	SON OR DAUGHTER LEAVING HOME	29	_____
24.	TROUBLE WITH IN-LAWS	29	_____
25.	OUTSTANDING PERSONAL ACHIEVEMENT	28	_____
26.	SPOUSE BEGINS OR STOPS WORK	28	_____
27.	STARTING OR FINISHING SCHOOL	28	_____
28.	CHANGE IN LIVING CONDITIONS	25	_____
29.	REVISION OF PERSONAL HABITS	24	_____
30.	TROUBLE WITH BOSS	23	_____
31.	CHANGE IN WORK HOURS, CONDITIONS	20	_____
32.	CHANGE IN RESIDENCE	20	_____
33.	CHANGE IN SCHOOLS	20	_____
34.	CHANGE IN RECREATIONAL HABITS	19	_____
35.	CHANGE IN CHURCH ACTIVITIES	19	_____
36.	CHANGE IN SOCIAL ACTIVITIES	18	_____
37.	MORTGAGE OR LOAN UNDER $50,000	17	_____
38.	CHANGE IN SLEEPING HABITS	16	_____
39.	CHANGE IN NUMBER OF FAMILY GATHERINGS	15	_____
40.	CHANGE IN EATING HABITS	15	_____
41.	VACATION	13	_____
42.	CHRISTMAS/MAJOR HOLIDAY SEASON	12	_____
43.	MINOR VIOLATION OF THE LAW	11	_____

TOTAL _____

SOURCE: DRS. THOMAS H. HOLMES AND RICHARD H. ROHE, UNIVERSITY OF WASHINGTON MEDICAL SCHOOL.

Figure 3

So, how did you do? Before you get overconfident because your score was so low, or become concerned because your score was so high, let's take this a little bit further. There are forty-three *major* life events on this list, but what about all the *little* hassles you encounter every day? Richard Lazarus, Professor of Psychology at the University of California at Berkeley, did a study that proved the small defeats and troubles in our daily lives cause as much harm as the big ones. Hassles are the irritating, frustrating, or distressing incidents that occur in the everyday transactions with our environment. They can take the form of disagreements, disappointments, accidents, or unpleasant surprises. They may range from getting stuck in traffic to losing a wallet, from an argument with your teenager to a dispute with your boss. The more frequent and intense the hassles people reported, the poorer their overall mental and physical health was reported to be. *Why?* Constant, "small" hassles don't give us time to recoup between the experiences of stressors. Most of the time it's not the *amount* of stress that is so harmful; it's our inability to *control* the stress. We must learn how to distinguish between *avoidable* and *unavoidable* stress and to be able, at times, to just *let things go.*

If I held out a glass of water in my hand toward you and asked, "How heavy is this glass of water?" you might say, "Six-to-twelve ounces." But the actual weight of the water doesn't matter (in regard to the stress incurred in me by holding it forward). This depends on *how long* I try to do so. If I hold it for a minute, that's not a problem. If I hold it for an hour, I'll have an ache in my arm. If I hold it for a day, you'll have to call an ambulance! In each case, the glass is the same weight, but the longer I hold it, the heavier it becomes.

Likewise, if we carry our burdens *all* the time, then sooner or later, as the burden becomes increasingly heavy, we won't be able to carry on. Yet, when we are refreshed at intervals, we can carry on again and again. I believe you will also find, as you continue with these assessments, that what is stress-relieving for one person can be stress-producing for another. For example: a divorce (number two on the life-events survey list) can be absolutely devastating to a person who thought she or he had a good marriage, and yet a tremendous relief for someone trapped in an abusive or negative relationship.

Preparing for Christmas or other major holidays, at the bottom of the life events list, can be a source of exhilaration for those who are looking forward to spending time with loved ones they don't see often. However, for those who are estranged from family, and/or those who just lost a close family member, the holiday season can be a very stressful and depressing time. Psychological stress resides neither in the *situation* nor the *person*: it depends on a transaction between the two. It arises from how the person appraises an event and adapts to it.

> Psychological stress resides neither in the situation nor the person: it depends on a transaction between the two. It arises from how the person appraises an event and adapts to it.

The previous assessment covered forty-three major life events measured over the space of two years. Now let's look at the things that have caused you any amount of stress during the past week.

DAY-TO-DAY STRESS INVENTORY

LIST ALL THE THINGS THAT CAUSED ANY AMOUNT OF STRESS FOR YOU
IN THE LAST WEEK:

1. _____	11. _____
2. _____	12. _____
3. _____	13. _____
4. _____	14. _____
5. _____	15. _____
6. _____	16. _____
7. _____	17. _____
8. _____	18. _____
9. _____	19. _____
10. _____	20. _____

ADD THE NUMBER OF CAUSES FROM THE ABOVE RELATING TO:

A.	_____	YOUR JOB, CAREER, OR PROFESSIONAL LIFE
B.	_____	YOUR MARRIAGE, FAMILY LIFE, CHILDREN
C.	_____	FRIENDS, SOCIAL COMMITMENTS
D.	_____	PERSONAL HEALTH
E.	_____	FINANCES, INCOME, DEBT
F.	_____	SELF-PERCEPTION, ESTEEM, PURPOSE, PRIORITIES, ACCOMPLISHMENTS
G.	_____	OTHER (EG, TRAFFIC, CAR TROUBLE, LOST KEYS ...)

Figure 4

When you looked at the causes, based on the seven categories at the bottom of the assessment (A–G), did you notice a concentration of stress occurring in one or two areas? We will revisit this strong probability as we go deeper into the assessments. As I mentioned before, we all have different tolerances for stress. Please take this next test to determine your own Tolerance Profile.

STRESS TOLERANCE PROFILE

ASSESS YOUR ABILITY TO COPE WITH STRESS. BE CANDID. CHECK THE MOST
REALISTIC FREQUENCY FOR EACH STATEMENT.

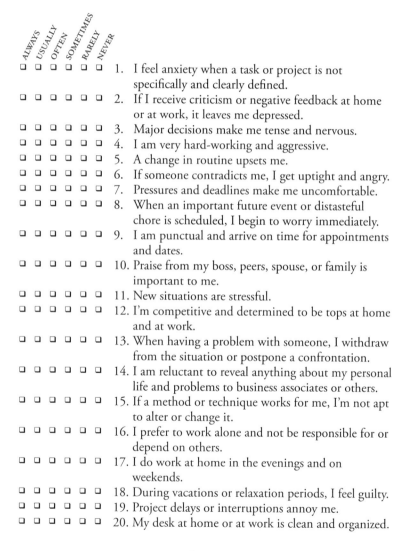

ALWAYS USUALLY OFTEN SOMETIMES RARELY NEVER

1. I feel anxiety when a task or project is not specifically and clearly defined.

2. If I receive criticism or negative feedback at home or at work, it leaves me depressed.

3. Major decisions make me tense and nervous.

4. I am very hard-working and aggressive.

5. A change in routine upsets me.

6. If someone contradicts me, I get uptight and angry.

7. Pressures and deadlines make me uncomfortable.

8. When an important future event or distasteful chore is scheduled, I begin to worry immediately.

9. I am punctual and arrive on time for appointments and dates.

10. Praise from my boss, peers, spouse, or family is important to me.

11. New situations are stressful.

12. I'm competitive and determined to be tops at home and at work.

13. When having a problem with someone, I withdraw from the situation or postpone a confrontation.

14. I am reluctant to reveal anything about my personal life and problems to business associates or others.

15. If a method or technique works for me, I'm not apt to alter or change it.

16. I prefer to work alone and not be responsible for or depend on others.

17. I do work at home in the evenings and on weekends.

18. During vacations or relaxation periods, I feel guilty.

19. Project delays or interruptions annoy me.

20. My desk at home or at work is clean and organized.

Figure 5

STRESS TOLERANCE PROFILE INTERPRETATION

NOW THAT YOU'VE COMPLETED THE STRESS TOLERANCE PROFILE, LET'S TRANSLATE YOUR SELF EVALUATION INTO A WEIGHTED POINT-SCORE. FIRST ADD UP THE TOTAL CHECKS IN EACH OF THE SIX COLUMNS, AND MULTIPLY EACH TOTAL BY THE POINT ALLOCATIONS SHOWN IN THE CHART BELOW. ENTER YOUR COLUMN TOTALS IN THE APPROPRIATE BLANKS AND SIMPLY MULTIPLY THE TOTAL CHECKS BY THE POINT ALLOCATION FOR EACH FREQUENCY. FINALLY, ADD ALL THE EXTENDED TOTALS TO ARRIVE AT YOUR SCORE.

FREQUENCY	TOTAL CHECKS	POINT ALLOCATIONS		POINT TOTALS
ALWAYS	(_____	X 5	POINTS)	= _____
USUALLY	(_____	X 4	POINTS)	= _____
OFTEN	(_____	X 3	POINTS)	= _____
SOMETIMES	(_____	X 2	POINTS)	= _____
RARELY	(_____	X 1	POINTS)	= _____
NEVER	(_____	X 0	POINTS)	= _____

HERE'S HOW TO INTERPRET YOUR SCORE, WHICH REPRESENTS A REASONABLE APPROXIMATION OF YOUR STRESS THRESHOLD, OR YOUR ABILITY TO WITHSTAND STRESS. IF YOUR SCORE IS UNDER 50 POINTS, YOU HAVE A LOW-STRESS PROFILE AND CAN PROBABLY HANDLE STRESS QUITE HANDILY. ON THE OTHER HAND, IF YOUR SCORE WAS OVER 50, IT INDICATES THAT YOU HAVE A HIGH-STRESS PROFILE AND ARE SOMEWHAT STRESS-PRONE. THE FURTHER YOUR SCORE IS FROM THE MID-POINT (50), THE MORE EXTREME IS YOUR REACTION TO STRESS. FOR EXAMPLE, A 75 WOULD BE A HIGHLY STRESSED PERSON, AND A 25 WOULD DESCRIBE SOMEONE WHO IS VERY LOW-STRESSED AND COULD HANDLE SUBSTANTIAL AMOUNTS OF TENSION AND PRESSURE.

Figure 5 (Continued)

Obviously, this is not a foolproof measure of your ability to deal with stress. However, it's useful in approximating your stress threshold and serves as another indicator of the way in which you personally handle stress.

Many of you have heard about "Type A" and "Type B" personality research. Cardiologists Dr. Rosenman and Dr. Friedman began working on a project back in the 1970s, seeking to detect human behaviors that might lead to heart attacks. They concluded from their study that: "'Type A' personalities are three times more likely to develop heart disease than 'Type B' personalities." Type A's, they said, pursue a chronic, incessant struggle to achieve more and more in less and less time. They constantly compete, challenging themselves and others, and thrive on deadlines, creating them if they don't exist. Usually they are highly status-oriented.

Type B's are creative, imaginative, and philosophical. They are rarely harried by desire to do more and more in less and less time. They are contemplative and ponder alternatives and like to work at their own pace. They feel they know the real meaning of life.

This next assessment is a Lifestyle Questionnaire that can be useful in determining how much of a Type A and /or Type B personality you have and how it can affect your health.

LIFESTYLE QUESTIONNAIRE

BELOW IS A GROUP OF STATEMENTS RELATED TO EVERYDAY LIVING. PLEASE INDICATE, ON A SCALE OF 1 TO 5 (SCALE VALUES BELOW), THE DEGREE TO WHICH EACH IS PERSONALLY APPLICABLE:

1 = NEVER; 2 = RARELY; 3 = SOMETIMES; 4 = FREQUENTLY; 5 = ALWAYS

_____ 1. I want to be the best at everything I do.
_____ 2. I get annoyed in traffic jams.
_____ 3. I become impatient when waiting in line.
_____ 4. I find myself getting angry if kept waiting for an appointment.
_____ 5. I like to drive my car very fast.
_____ 6. Meeting new acquaintances is very stressful for me.
_____ 7. I get angry with co-workers who are inefficient.
_____ 8. I find I try harder than others to accomplish things.
_____ 9. I seem to put more effort into my job than other people.
_____ 10. My spouse or friends think I am hard-driving and work too hard.
_____ 11. I get irritable when others don't take their job seriously.
_____ 12. I am determined to win when playing a game with friends.
_____ 13. I enjoy intense competition.
_____ 14. When playing a game with a child, I will purposely let him win.
_____ 15. I move, walk, talk, and eat rapidly.
_____ 16. I feel impatient because most things happen too slowly.
_____ 17. I think about business constantly.
_____ 18. I feel guilty when I relax or take it easy.
_____ 19. I challenge people about their thoughts or ideas.
_____ 20. I rely more on other people's opinions than on my own.
_____ 21. I seem to have little spare time.
_____ 22. I do my work faster and more efficiently than my co-worker.
_____ 23. I enjoy discussing my achievements.
_____ 24. I become angry easily with my spouse or friends.
_____ 25. I personally do not reveal things about myself.
_____ 26. I find that I am quiet or subdued.
_____ 27. I appear more aggressive than others.
_____ 28. I let others know it when I am angry.
_____ 29. I find I have insufficient time in which to finish my work.
_____ 30. I become confused when too many things happen at once.
_____ 31. I wish I had help to get things done.
_____ 32. Because of my work, I have no opportunity to do the things I really want to do in life.
_____ 33. I rely only on myself to get things done.
_____ 34. Relaxing seems to infringe on my work time.
_____ 35. I skip meals to get things done.
_____ 36. I do extra work to impress others.
_____ 37. I seem to race against the clock to save time.
_____ 38. Luck has a great deal to do with success.
_____ 39. I lose my temper under pressure.
_____ 40. I make mistakes because I feel rushed into things without thinking them through completely.

SOURCE: DRS. ROSENMAN AND FRIEDMAN.

Figure 6

LIFESTYLE QUESTIONNAIRE SCORING

ADD UP THE NUMERIC VALUE (1-5) FOR EACH STATEMENT ON THE QUESTIONNAIRE TO DETERMINE YOUR TOTAL SCORE.

TOTAL SCORE = 168–200 TYPE A1	IF YOU ARE IN THIS CATEGORY, AND ESPECIALLY IF YOU ARE OVER 40 AND SMOKE, YOU ARE LIKELY TO HAVE A HIGH RISK OF DEVELOPING CARDIAC ILLNESS.
TOTAL SCORE = 136–168 TYPE A2	YOU ARE IN THE DIRECTION OF BEING CARDIAC-PRONE, BUT YOUR RISK IS NOT AS HIGH AS THE A1. YOU SHOULD, NEVERTHELESS, PAY CAREFUL ATTENTION TO THE ADVICE GIVEN TO ALL TYPE A'S.
TOTAL SCORE = 104–136 TYPE AB	YOU ARE A MIXTURE OF A AND B PATTERNS. THIS IS A HEALTHIER PATTERN THAN EITHER A1 OR A2, BUT YOU HAVE THE POTENTIAL FOR SLIPPING INTO "A" BEHAVIOR AND YOU SHOULD RECOGNIZE THIS.
TOTAL SCORE = 72–104 TYPE B2	YOUR BEHAVIOR IS ON THE LESS-CARDIAC-PRONE END OF THE SPECTRUM. YOU ARE GENERALLY RELAXED AND COPE ADEQUATELY WITH STRESS.
TOTAL SCORE = 40–72 TYPE B1	YOU TEND TO THE EXTREME OF NON-CARDIAC TRAITS. YOUR BEHAVIOR EXPRESSES FEW OF THE REACTIONS ASSOCIATED WITH CARDIAC DISEASE.

Figure 6 (Continued)

Now you know where you stand in our discussion of Type A and Type B behaviors. The higher your score, the more cardiac-prone you tend to be. Remember, though, even Type B persons occasionally slip into Type A behavior, and any of these patterns can change over time. Dr. Friedman asserted that he is not trying to change personalities, but to eliminate what he sees as the *destructive side* of being a Type A: the struggle against time and other people, which creates the hormonal disturbances that lead to disease. A person can be a Type A but not struggle. A tiger asleep is the same as a lamb asleep. It's when he awakens that the trouble begins.

Now, as a result of the previous four assessments, you have a general idea about your overall stress index based on major life events, what causes your day–to–day stress, your stress tolerance profile, and your basic personality type. It's time to go deeper, using a different lens, to survey perspectives on seven life dimensions in order to better understand the specific stressors that affect you most.

CHAPTER THREE

SEVEN KEY LIFE DIMENSIONS

"We do not grow absolutely, chronologically.
We grow sometimes in one dimension and not in another.
We are mature in one realm, childish in another."

—Anais Nin

To truly understand personal stress and to make your life more fulfilling and enjoyable, you must identify the specific sources of stress in *your* life. I have identified seven key dimensions in life that I believe, collectively, construct a useful profile of one's unique identity and level of self-esteem. Let's briefly explore each one.

THE SEVEN KEY LIFE DIMENSIONS

Figure 7

Dimension I: Family

I list this dimension first because it can have such a major impact on our lives—as a source of either comfort or stress. Obviously, life begins with our first relationships: our parents, grandparents, aunts/uncles, and siblings, as each of us is uniquely given. In a life fraught with so much uncertainty and heartache, many believe we should find the greatest support and love from our family. And yet, family can also produce the most stressful and emotionally-charged, negative relationships in your overall life experience. Living with others is stressful in itself, whether it's with toddlers who are into everything or teens (who are also into everything!). Maybe you're not living up to your parents' expectations. Maybe you aren't living up to your spouse's expectations, either. Or maybe you're so caught up in your own struggle to be successful you've forgotten to keep in touch with the people who got you where you are, the people who gave you the confidence to conquer the world, or those who brought you into this world. None of those situations feels good.

For those who marry and have children, there are two families; the one we're born into and the one we build. As that new family expands and we add spouses, in-laws, ex-spouses, stepchildren, half brothers, ex-in-laws, etc., the stress often expands exponentially in proportion to the number of complex relationships we're managing. Today, fifty percent of first marriages end in divorce (though that percentage is dropping slightly as I write this), and the divorce rate in second marriages is even higher. This is due partly to people not learning from their mistakes and remarrying the same type of person, or not looking inside themselves to see where *they* need to change before they change partners. If it was a death rather than a divorce that made your new spouse single again, then you don't have a living husband or wife to deal with, but competing with their memory can be almost as difficult.

Families in the 50s, 60s, and 70s could never live up to the popular television programs of their day about family: *Father Knows Best, Ozzie and Harriet* (no, not *The* [Ozzie] *Osbournes*—that's Generation X's family model), and *The Brady Bunch*. Everything in these families was perfect, and if there ever *was* a small crisis, it always ended well . . . magically resolved inside of thirty minutes! Those shows made our *real* families feel like they fell far short by comparison, as we set our expectations of family life too high.

Often we expect family members to give unconditional love, but frequently the only guarantee of unconditional love comes from the family dog. When we left our golden retriever, Brandy, home alone all day, at night when we returned home he was always filled with complete joy, jumping with excitement to see us. I can never remember our teenagers doing that!

And yet, despite all this family stress, for some reason (statistically speaking) married men live eight years longer than single men and ten years longer than widowers. Married women live three years longer than single women and four years longer than widows. Go figure!

Make a list of the family members, immediate and extended, whom you see at least a few times a year. Then put a plus (+) mark next to the people who make you feel good, increase your self esteem, stimulate you, help you grow, and make you laugh and enjoy life more. Put a minus (-) next to the names of people who have a negative effect on you, bore you, cause you to question your self worth, make you feel angry, depressed, or anxious . . . anyone who leaves you feeling drained and frustrated. Put a "0" beside names of neutral people, those who neither add nor detract from your life. Some of these people may grow to be plusses as you get to know them better or spend more time with them—or they could grow to be minuses.

Family Assessment

NAME	EFFECT (+, -, o)	NAME	EFFECT (+, -, o)

Figure 8

As you think through your relationships with family members, consider some of the following questions:

- Overall, is your family close, and does it serve as a positive support mechanism for you? Or is it a constant source of conflict?

- Are your parents (if still alive) a source of unconditional love and encouragement, or are they a source of anxiety, as you don't ever seem to measure up?

- Is your spouse a true life partner and friend, sharing in your joys and sorrows and being supportive, or a source of negative emotions?

- Are your kids (if you have kids) a source of pride and joy or a source of constant concern, frustration, and heartache?

- Is your extended family, including in-laws, ex's, and more distant members, a source of positive or negative feelings? Or, are your emotions about these relatives neither positive nor negative?

Now, after reflecting on all of this, please rate your level of satisfaction and fulfillment with your *family dimension* (on a scale of one to five):

1: A source of major dissatisfaction and stress.

2: A source of some dissatisfaction and stress.

3: Neutral, neither positive, nor negative.

4: A source of satisfaction and fulfillment.

5: A source of great satisfaction and fulfillment.

Dimension II: Social

This dimension encompasses all of your *other* relationships beyond family (your friends, neighbors, and coworkers). It also includes your role and interdependence with the world around you—from the local community, your state, country, and the world at large, including the natural environment. Our social endeavors also include leisure time activities such as hobbies, clubs, sports, and other interests—especially those in which we interact with others. You may feel so passionate about one of your interests that it almost defines your purpose in life, even if it's just an avocation and not your profession. Obviously, all of these social elements can be important in *managing* stress or in *causing* stress. An argument with a close friend or coworker, a major setback or loss of a political campaign, or being left off of an invitation list to a significant social event can be devastating if being a part of these is truly important to you.

A landmark UCLA study by Gale Berkowitz suggested that friendships between women are special. They shape who we are and who we are yet to be. They soothe our tumultuous inner world, fill the emotional gaps in our marriages, and help us remember who we really are. By the way, they may do even more than this. Scientists now suspect that hanging out with friends can actually counteract the kind of stomach-quivering stress most of us experience on a daily basis.

One study suggests that women respond to stress with a cascade of brain chemicals that causes them to make and maintain

> Most of us tend to judge others by their behavior and ourselves by our intentions.

friendships with other women. It seems that when the hormone *oxytocin* is released as part of the stress responses in women, it can buffer the "fight or flight" response, and it can encourage them to tend children and gather with other women. When a woman does this *tending or befriending,* studies suggest that more oxytocin is released, and that further counters stress and produces a calming effect. This calming response does not occur in men, says Dr. Laura Klein, an assistant professor of bio-behavioral health at Pennsylvania State University. That's because testosterone, which men produce in high levels when they're under stress, seems to reduce the effects of oxytocin. Estrogen seems to enhance it. *Could this be one of the reasons women outlive men?*

Study after study has found that social ties reduce our risk of disease by lowering blood pressure, heart rate, and cholesterol. When the UCLA study looked at how well the women functioned after the death of a spouse, they found that even in the face of this huge stress, those women who had a close friend and confidante were more likely to survive the experience without any new physical impairments or permanent loss of vitality.

So, if friends counter the stress that seems to swallow up so much of our lives these days, if they keep us healthy and even add years to our lives, why is it so hard to find time to be with them? Sometimes, when we get overly busy with work and family, the first thing we do is let go of friendships. That's really a mistake, because women are a necessary and vital source of strength to one another.

USA Today snapshots women's top priorities	
#1 More time with family and friends	68%
#2 Eat healthier	28%
#3 Reduce stress	27%
#4 Get in better shape	22%
#5 Reduced debt	21%
#6 Lose Weight	20%
#7 Find a new career	8%

To begin, we are going to take the same assessment we used with our family members, assessing the impact each of our friends and coworkers has upon us. Again, mark each name with a +, -, or 0 to reflect their impact on you.

Now, on a blank sheet of paper (or in your journal or notebook), make a list of all your leisure activities . . . including current hobbies, interests, clubs, sports, social activities, political involvement, and so on. Assess each of these with the same

SOCIAL ASSESSMENT

NAME	EFFECT (+, -, 0)	NAME	EFFECT (+, -, 0)

Figure 9

"+, -, or 0" to reflect the value they provide to you. Think about the activities you may now be trapped in that no longer provide satisfaction. Then build a list of new activities you'd love to do or at least *try* but haven't yet found time to pursue.

To evaluate your overall satisfaction with this area of your life, you should think about the following questions:

- Are the relationships with your close friends supportive and nurturing—or draining and frustrating?

- Do your friends share your life values and passions? Have you changed, or have they?

- Do you enjoy spending time with coworkers, or are they a detriment to your work environment?

- Are your current leisure activities and hobbies truly fulfilling, or are they more like obligations or habits you've outgrown?

- Are there new activities you think would be exciting to pursue?

As in the previous life dimension, rank your social life in terms of personal fulfillment and satisfaction using the following scale:

1: A source of major dissatisfaction and stress.

2: A source of some dissatisfaction and stress.

3: Neutral, neither positive, nor negative.

4: A source of satisfaction and fulfillment.

5: A source of great satisfaction and fulfillment.

Dimension III: Career

Most of us spend more than half of our waking hours at our jobs, so it's no surprise that our career satisfaction can have a positive impact on our fulfillment and happiness or be a serious source of stress. This dimension encompasses the personal satisfaction you get from your occupation, beginning with career choice, meaningful work, effective use of your talents and skills, career path progress, and personal performance.

Do you feel you have a career, or just a job? Maybe it's just not going where you expected it would ten or twenty years ago. Maybe your ambition got thwarted along the way with bad managers or bad luck. Maybe you were over-promoted or under-promoted. (Why do I suspect most of you are thinking you've been under-promoted?) Maybe you regret not going to college, law school, or art school when you were younger, and now it seems too late since you'd be in your 40s by the time you got your degree. *So what?* You're going to be in your 40s anyway, so why not be there with your degree?

Career stress can affect everyone and at every age. If you're young, what's the right career choice, and how do you get into that field? If you're more seasoned, how do you continue to add value to your work and remain competitive and productive? How do you reconcile the conflicting needs of work and family, and how do you earn enough to support a family without compromising your own happiness and fulfillment? As a son or daughter, how do you reconcile your own career choices with what your parents may want for you? For example, did your dad have a business he wanted you to take over when you graduated from college, but you had no desire to do that? Or did you only *wish* your dad had a business you could take over since you had no strong direction in what you wanted to do as a career?

Occupational and work-related stress has been a well-documented, global phenomenon for decades. A recent study in the UK found that two thirds of public sector employees and half of employees in the private sector were experiencing high stress at work. Sources of stress cited included: poor working conditions, relationships at work, an unclear role of the organization, long hours, lack of job security, organizational climate, and a general mismatch between individual personality type and the requirements of the job. In the public sector, the most stressed professionals are teachers, social workers, prison employees, and police. At the other end of the wage scale, a Harvard Medical School study found that nearly 18 percent of a sample group of 12,000 physicians were dissatisfied and did not find medicine to be a fulfilling career. Issues cited include lack of autonomy, health insurance restrictions, lack of time to spend with patients, and little opportunity for continuing relationships with patients.

Career-related stress and dissatisfaction has become so prevalent that a formal field of study has emerged within psychology called the Career Depression Syndrome (CDS). CDS entails three stages: The first stage is merely career dissatisfaction, something we may all identify with at times, but it can last six months or more. In the second stage, you may experience a lack of motivation, indicated by frequent absences or poor job performance. Employees here may still be making a good living and have career security, but they feel depressed about their occupation. The third stage of CDS is paralysis, a feeling of fear, hopelessness, and inadequacy, which often keeps people from taking positive steps to change jobs. By this stage, the entire family and social life have often been impacted. In a climate of downsizing and overall career uncertainty, exacerbated by changes in technology and a more fast-paced society, CDS is considered by many professionals to be epidemic.

As you reflect on the career dimension of your life, consider these questions:

- Have you selected the right career, one that you're sincerely interested in and even *passionate* about, or did you end up here by circumstance? Are your skills a good fit for your career?

- Are you satisfied with the firm you work for? Do you enjoy the overall work climate, working conditions, coworkers, and your personal work space?

- Do you have a career path in mind, and are you progressing successfully on it? Do you believe you're fairly compensated for the value of the work you provide?

- Does your immediate manager respect you, value you, and recognize your performance?

- Do you see any signs of Career Depression Syndrome— de-motivation, declining performance, or frequent absences?

Now, assess your overall sense of personal fulfillment and satisfaction with your career. Is it:

1: A source of major dissatisfaction and stress.

2: A source of some dissatisfaction and stress.

3: Neutral, neither positive, nor negative.

4: A source of satisfaction and fulfillment.

5: A source of great satisfaction and fulfillment.

Dimension IV: Spiritual

The spiritual dimension is about your search for meaning and purpose, a sense of self, and that which is greater than self. It's about your beliefs and values and the consistency with which you live your life. Spirituality is most frequently a stress reliever, as spiritual activities serve to renew, lift up, comfort, heal, and inspire us. Do you have a need for a spiritual journey at this time in your life? If you do, where are you in your spiritual journey? Are you moving closer to the God you believe in, or farther away? If you feel *farther away*, then ask yourself, who moved?

Is the concept of God ethereal to you? Do you believe a Supreme Being, Creator, or Higher Power is out there, but you don't feel closely connected to that One through a personal relationship? Do you go to church or synagogue, yet don't feel the need to pray and commune with God on a daily basis? Do you feel that your values and principles are becoming better formed with age and that you're living them as fully as possible, or are you compromising your values and ethics? Do you find inner peace, joy, harmony, and contentment through your faith, or do you worry about everything, not trusting in God to get you through what He brought you to?

At different points in our lives we find a smaller or greater need to be in touch with our Creator. Many of us were raised in a faith, and when we grew up and went to college we turned away from faith, only to return to it after we had our own family or after a major crisis. According to current market research on this subject, 93 percent of people in the U.S. believe in God. Coincidentally, back in 1994, a *US News and World Report* article gave the same percentage the new research reported: 93 percent are believers. That same study showed that 60 percent hold to their parents' religious beliefs, and more than 80 percent believe the Bible is the inspired Word of God (including 71 percent of college graduates). A CNN Gallup poll published recently in *USA Today* said that 59 percent state faith is "important" to them, and another 29 percent state that it is "fairly important." But the key question to me is: "Does a person's faith help him or her through stressful events in life?" My master's thesis focused on that very topic.

As you can see by now, there is a pattern to my passion. My hypothesis: People who have a high degree of spirituality, evidenced by a strong, personal relationship with God, are better able to cope with high–stress–producing, uncontrollable life events. I won't spend the time here to go through the thesis in detail, but I will touch on its highlights. Those in my research sample who had a *very strong* personal relationship with God felt they could cope much better; those who were lukewarm or *weren't sure* about their faith in God and whether or not they were "good enough" to go to heaven, were not able to cope well. Also, surprisingly to me, those who were at the opposite end of the spectrum, who had no personal faith, were able to deal with uncontrollable life stress almost as well as those that had a deep belief.

After extensive research and in-depth interviews, I concluded that those with deep faith were able to get through serious life events, like the death of someone close, because of the peace their faith in God brought them and the knowledge that their loved one was in heaven. Those who had *no* real faith in God and lost a loved one decided they had to continue on and make the best of this life because of their belief that this life is really all there is.

DEEP FAITH HELPS IN COPING WITH STRESS

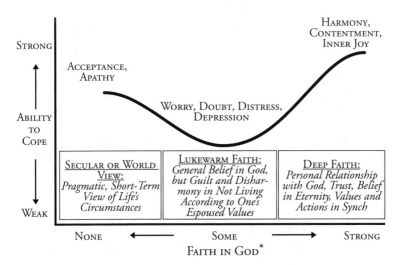

*MEASURED BY FREQUENCY OF PRAYER, SERVICE ATTENDANCE, SCRIPTURE READING, EXTENT OF CHURCH/TEMPLE INVOLVEMENT, DEGREE THAT GOD ANSWERS PRAYER, BELIEF THAT GOD CONTROLS LIFE EVENTS.

Figure 10

Study Demographics: 44 total respondents

Gender: 24 female, 16 male, 4 unspecified

Marital status: 25 married, 12 single, 5 divorced, 2 widowed

Religion: 18 Roman Catholic (4 non-practicing), 17 Protestant (5 born again Christians), 6 Jewish, 1 Greek Orthodox, 2 Agnostic

Age: 5 in 20s, 6 in 30s, 17 in 40s, 11 in 50s, 1 in 60s, 1 in 70s, 3 unspecified

Here are some questions to think about as you rate your fulfillment in this key area of life:

- How strong is your faith in God? Is it a close, personal relationship? Is it strengthening or weakening over time as you encounter each of life's challenges?

- Do you find that your faith reduces your anxiety, comforts you, and creates inner joy . . . or do you feel more negative emotions of guilt, worry, or even apathy?

- To what extent are you living your life according to your value system, beliefs, and faith? Are you "walking the talk," actively demonstrating your faith in God each day?

- To what extent are you in harmony with your spouse in this area? To quote the Bible, are you "equally yoked?"

- Are you getting support from close family and friends who share your faith? And are you successfully encouraging others close to you, including your children, to strengthen their faith in God?

So, now rank your overall satisfaction and fulfillment with the spirituality and faith dimension of your life. Is it:

1: A source of major dissatisfaction and stress.

2: A source of some dissatisfaction and stress.

3: Neutral, neither positive, nor negative.

4: A source of satisfaction and fulfillment.

5: A source of great satisfaction and fulfillment.

Dimension V: Health—Physical and Mental

This dimension entails taking personal responsibility for your health and wellness, including diet, nutrition, exercise, and medical care. Building physical strength and endurance can certainly be an important stress-reducing activity. But as we've discussed, there's a close mind-body connection. I don't know about you, but every time I have a headache for more than a few days in a row, I'm sure I have a brain tumor! Also, the media provides us with so much "valuable" information on our diet and supplements. One day eggs will kill us; the next day they are good for us. Every few months I read completely conflicting data on hormone replacement therapy. One report says it keeps me young and protects my heart and brain from Alzheimer's, and the next, says just the opposite.

You not only have your own health to be concerned about, but also the health of your family members and close friends. As previously mentioned, the mind and body are more than married, they are intimately united; when one suffers the other sympathizes. If you are upset for a long period of time over the way you have been treated by a loved one or are worried "sick" about losing your job or are anxious a great deal about your child's future, your body will begin to feel that mental stress and make you physically sick. Also, when you are very sick for a long period of time, your mind can begin to get depressed and discouraged. Just trying to understand medical insurance rules about when and how to get professional help can be stressful in and of itself!

Being *fit* and being *well* are terms that describe totally different conditions. However, both are essential to maintaining your health. Wellness depends on your immune system and nutrition, sometimes using the assistance of vitamins and supplements. Some people who are fit can be unwell, and some well people can be unfit. When you combine the two and use sound principles based on clean living, exercise, and healthy eating, you attain a state of balance that helps you to maintain both fitness and wellness. Needless to say, you have probably heard *somewhere* about what you should be eating to maintain your health and what type of exercise you should be doing, as well as how long you should be doing it, to maintain your best fitness level. *Are you listening?*

> The mind and body are more than married, they are intimately united; when one suffers, the other sympathizes.

Every researcher and fitness guru agrees that exercise is the one thing that is good for everyone. The case for exercise and health has primarily been made due to its impact on physical diseases; specifically coronary heart disease, obesity, and diabetes. In the last fifteen years there has been increasing research into the role of exercise in the treatment of mental health and in improving mental well-being in the general population. There is good evidence that aerobic and resistance exercises enhance mood states, and there is evidence that exercise can improve cognitive function in older adults. The use of physical activity can be a means of upgrading the quality of life through enhanced self-esteem, improved mood states, increased resilience to stress, and improved sleep.

Some questions to think about as you rate your satisfaction and fulfillment levels regarding your mental and physical health are:

- Are you physically fit? Have you established a regular exercise program that includes aerobic and weight training activity?

- Do you have a balanced, healthy diet? Are you overweight or underweight?

- Do you go to the doctor for medical checkups at least once a year?

- Are you getting the right amount of sleep, and do you wake up feeling refreshed?

- How is your mental state? Are you depressed, nervous, or do you have a high level of anxiety much of the time? Or are you relatively happy, contented, and at peace with yourself?

As with the previous dimensions, rank your physical and mental health in terms of personal fulfillment and satisfaction:

1: A source of major dissatisfaction and stress.

2: A source of some dissatisfaction and stress.

3: Neutral, neither positive, nor negative.

4: A source of satisfaction and fulfillment.

5: A source of great satisfaction and fulfillment.

Dimension VI: Intellectual

This dimension is about creativity and mental stimulation. To what extent are you mentally challenged and growing your brain cells, which are purportedly dying at a rate of a billion a year? Are you actively expanding your knowledge and skill base, either in the classroom or beyond, using cultural activities? How do you now learn about and keep abreast of current issues: through books, magazines, newspapers, the Internet, TV, or lectures? How do you develop your intellectual curiosity and stretch your mind? Do you pursue mind-strengthening games such as chess, bridge, or crossword puzzles? Do you have regrets over not pursuing more formal education, and is that one of the things that seems to stymie your ability to work in a profession that is more stimulating and energizing? Are you being creatively challenged in your job or hobbies, or do you feel mental boredom? As you age, does the natural deterioration associated with memory loss serve as a new source of stress?

The French used to say that life is divided into three phases: learning, working, and living. That no longer holds true in this Information Age. Learning, working, and living now all occur simultaneously—and continue throughout life. So, intellectual stimulation is critically important to our life, health, and fulfillment. Studies now show that neurons and brain cells that deteriorate during life can be regenerated through mental activity. And longevity itself may be as influenced by our mental attitudes and stimu-lation as by our exercise, diet, and genetics. Now that learning is perceived to be a life-long endeavor, many community

> Learning, working, and living now all occur simultaneously—and continue throughout life.

colleges, high schools, and online universities have stepped up to provide the courseware for adult education.

The axiom, "You can't teach an old dog new tricks," is clearly out the window. Working men and women need to keep their skills sharp in order to remain competitive. Retirees, who often miss the mental aspects of their jobs, finally have time for new learning and the chance to pursue fields of study unrelated to their careers.

One group that has always expressed their frustration with mental boredom is the stay-at-home moms, who often crave adult conversation and mental stimulation. Although it's more challenging to locate, there are many ways to find it. Take a class, whether you're working on a degree or learning a new hobby. A night out in community education can put you in touch with thoughtful new people, help you learn something new, or keep you current in your career skills while not working in business. Online courses make it possible to do this from home if you can't get out. Or, learn while your child learns by finding a topic you both love and studying it with him or her. Learn a new language and teach it to your child at the same time. We all need to acquire more media savvy. Why not switch the radio dial to "talk radio" and listen to intellectual debates or turn the TV channel to one with more stimulating content.

As you assess your own satisfaction and fulfillment with the intellectual dimension of your life consider the following:

- Do you have a lifelong education plan to pursue more formal education, or do you capitalize on local community education offerings, such as a lecture series?

- Have you learned a new skill or become deeply informed and involved in a new topic in the past year?

- Are you finding ways to stimulate your mind in positive ways as part of your daily routine via radio, TV, Internet, or other media channels?

- Do you enjoy reading, book clubs, games, puzzles, chess, etc.? Are you devoting sufficient time to these stimulating activities?

- Do you weave intellectual pursuits into your social life, turning dinner conversation or house parties into mind-growing activities?

Now rank your intellectual life in terms of personal fulfillment and satisfaction:

1: A source of major dissatisfaction and stress.

2: A source of some dissatisfaction and stress.

3: Neutral, neither positive, nor negative.

4: A source of satisfaction and fulfillment.

5: A source of great satisfaction and fulfillment.

Dimension VII: Financial

This dimension encompasses our approach and satisfaction with managing our money, both short and long-term. Unfortunately, conflict about money is one of the key reasons cited for divorce, and it is a *major* stressor. A typical worry list for couples is: Do we have a budget, and are we meeting it? Do we have adequate savings? Are my earning capacity and my spending habits in balance? Do my spouse and I share the same financial values and disciplines? Today, everything is "buy now, pay later," and since interest rates are low, why not buy a newer, bigger house? Those children need to be able to live like the rest of the kids in their school, right?

If you live in New York City, a preschool can cost as much as college—and it's just as hard to get in! School applications for a two or three-year-old ask how your child has dealt with the trauma in his or her life so far *(Would that be toilet training?)*, and how many languages does she or he speak *(Actually, they haven't mastered English yet!)*. Then they want to come visit to see what the child's home life is like and whether you, as parents, will "fit into" the school. *(Now you certainly have to buy that apartment on the Upper West Side you've been considering!)*

It's not surprising that financial differences are one of the top issues cited for divorce of young couples. And at the other extreme of life, it's now rare, in the white collar world anyway, to have a pension. Therefore you must ensure that you are saving and investing in those 401Ks for your retirement; but, oops, the first twenty years of savings already went toward the kids' college fund . . . and there isn't a big chance they will get a scholarship, what with their toilet training problem and lack of their English language skills!

In a 2007 survey by the Pew Research Center, the single most commonly reported problem facing American families was *not having enough money* and not *meeting expenses*. In fact, twice the number of people reported *money issues* rather than *personal health problems* as the key family issue. Financial worries range from keeping up with the cost of living, to high prices, to higher taxes and energy costs, to saving for retirement, to having enough money for health care and education. And the concerns increase among younger Americans, women, the undereducated, African American, and Hispanics. And according to a Citibank survey, 57 percent of divorced couples in the U.S. cited *financial problems* as the primary reason for the demise of their marriage. Financial incompatibility has a lot to do with how people are raised, their family traditions, and their role models.

Some questions to think about as you rate your satisfaction with the financial dimension of your life:

- Do you have a long-range investment plan to adequately provide for retirement, health care, and potential emergencies?

- Do you have a short term budget, and do you stick to it? Are your expenses and income roughly in balance?

- Do you and your spouse share the same financial values, approaches to saving, investing, and borrowing; and do you have similar tolerances for risk?

Now, after reflecting on all of this, please rate your current level of satisfaction and fulfillment in your financial dimension:

1: A source of major dissatisfaction and stress.

2: A source of some dissatisfaction and stress.

3: Neutral, neither positive, nor negative.

4: A source of satisfaction and fulfillment.

5: A source of great satisfaction and fulfillment.

Moving from Introspection to Action

Taken together these seven key dimensions define who we are, how we live our life, and how various life forces impact us. They feed directly into our self-perception. If you've taken the time to be truly reflective and to think through each of these, then you should be able to identify the one, two, or three that are currently causing you the most stress . . . and perhaps the two or three that are your greatest sources of joy. Now, let's lay out a personal action plan to make the commitment to change. That's the very next step. *Read on!*

CHAPTER FOUR

MAKING THE COMMITMENT TO CHANGE

"One cannot expect to solve a complex problem using the same level of consciousness that created that problem."
—Albert Einstein

During the course of your journey you will build several different action plans. At this stage, our focus will be on reducing or "starving" the stress. We can't just *complain* about it. Whining gets us nowhere. We have to act on the negative factors impacting our health, our joy, and our life. Some of these factors are truly life-threatening if we don't act on them and make the commitment to change.

Many of the pop culture solutions to stress are very general and unarguable, but not completely effective. They are typically "Band Aid®" or short-term fixes. "Eat better and exercise more!" *Wow!* What a novel concept! Of course, the things that relieve stress are unique and individual, because our stress is individual. What is stressful for you is not necessarily stressful for me, and what is stress-relieving for you may be stress-producing for me. For one person, shopping is a perfect elixir (until the bills come in), yet for another just driving past the mall is a stress-producer. One of you might want to jaunt off to a weekend retreat. For another, the idea of spontaneous travel causes anxiety.

Many of you probably love to garden when you are feeling stressed; that would be a stress-producer for me (given my *brown thumb*). Some like to go for walks, or go hiking, mountain climbing, or downhill skiing. Those could be terrifying for others. Some of us love to read or take a hot bath. Personally, the reading I love, but the hot bath I find totally boring. Some love to go for a car ride in the country, while others who are in their car all day for work or for taxiing children to activities would never look at driving as a stress reliever. People have hobbies (tennis, golf, knitting, collecting, woodworking, etc.) that they love, and so making time to do them is relaxing. Some stress relievers obviously are very bad for all of us: like smoking, excessive drinking, or using drugs—temporary solutions that, in time, could end up causing more long-term stress.

Of course, there are stress relievers that are important for all of us to do in some fashion: exercise, yoga, Pilates™, deep breathing, envisioning positive outcomes, praying, and having a good support system. Humor is wonderful for your health and psyche. Don't you feel terrific after you have laughed so hard that you cried? The release of tears, whether through laughter or sorrow, has been known to be a natural stress reliever. (I would rather laugh than cry, because my eyes swell up when I cry.)

One of the very best stress relievers is a concept called "altruistic egotism." Giving of yourself (your time, your talents, and your treasures) to others makes you feel good about yourself. No matter how bad things seem to be, you will always find people who are much worse off than you. When you are down and out, sad, or stressed, picking yourself up and doing something for those in need will lift you up. Now you have benefited at least two people: yourself and whomever you helped. As Madame De Maintenon, the 17th Century French educator, once said, "The true way to soften one's troubles is to solace those of others."

You may have done some of these things for others: cooking at a soup kitchen, helping children with their homework at a homeless shelter, helping the widow down the street put up her storm windows. Yes, *altruistic egotism* lifts our spirits. God knows what is good for us. After all being loving towards others is one of the two most important things God has commanded us to do. The first was ". . . and you shall love the Lord your

God with all your heart, with all your soul, with all your mind, and with all your strength. And the second is this, . . . love your neighbor as yourself. There is no other commandment greater than these" (Mark 12:29–30) (rsv).

In the pages that follow I will guide you to build specific action plans or strategies to address issues in each of the seven dimensions talked about in Chapter Three. Use these to build your own customized action plan and to find a good friend who knows you well and who can help support you in building and monitoring your personal action plan.

Did you ever notice that it's easier to diagnose and suggest actions to help other people than to assess and fix yourself? Let's look at someone else's life and see if we can propose a long-term and permanent solution to her issues.

Case Study: Susan and Mark Anthony

Susan Anthony could feel the anxiety building throughout her entire body as she tensed for the pending confrontation with her husband, Mark. For the third time this week she'd be arriving home late for dinner. The commute home felt more like three hours than the one-hour drive it really was. She had plenty of time to think about the problems in her life. With all the cutbacks the company had been going through, there was a lot more work for the people who were left. However, she knew she should be glad she still had her job, plus the overtime really helped the family financially. She just felt so overcommitted . . . work, family, church—each a big obligation and a major time commitment—with no clear options for escape!

Susan married Mark ten years ago, right after their graduation from Boston College. They were both so optimistic and delightfully surprised by the arrival of their first child, Elizabeth, after only one year of marriage. Not quite two years later, Lauren was born, and they were both happy, but Mark really wanted a boy so they tried again and, a year later, they had another daughter, Madeline. At that point, they decided *three kids* and two parents was the perfect family.

Susan wanted to stay at home with her children, at least until they were all in school full time. Then, out of the blue, Mark was laid off from his aircraft engineering position. This was more than a year ago, and the little bit of severance pay he was given was used up after six months. He had no luck finding a position worthy of his skills and education and was forced, for some income, to work part time helping a local carpenter. Despite sending out three hundred resumes, he believes his full-time career prospects will remain grim until the economy improves. Susan took a full-time secretarial position at a major corporation to obtain the medical benefits the family needed, plus money to help pay the mortgage. It's not the career Susan envisioned, but she hopes for promotional opportunities. She is working a great deal of overtime, because they are so short-staffed. The extra money comes in handy, but her new boss is very demanding and doesn't seem to care that sometimes she can't work overtime because of family obligations.

On a typical day, Susan's up at 5:30 A.M. and spends the first hour feeding, dressing, and talking to her children. By 7:15 she's had two cups of coffee and is on the road to work, as Mark takes over getting the kids to school and day care. After school he gathers up the kids and tries to do some needed chores, such as grocery shopping (always hoping no one he knows will see him) and cooking.

Two evenings a week Susan heads straight to the nursing home after work at 6 P.M. to visit her mother. Her mom began to deteriorate soon after her father's death two years ago, and the diagnosis was Alzheimer's disease. Susan took care of her until it was no longer feasible, but putting her mom in a nursing home was one of the hardest things she ever had to do. As an only child, Susan feels a heavy responsibility for her mom. Weekends are devoted to children, errands, housework, visiting her mom, church activities, and preparations for the week ahead. Susan and Mark joined a local church four years ago, both for their own and their children's spiritual well-being. Susan was raised in a church that didn't really teach the Bible, so she signed up for a Bible study one evening a week to help facilitate her new spiritual growth. Unfortunately, she's missed half the sessions because of schedule conflicts or sheer exhaustion.

Susan doesn't seem to have time to eat healthy or exercise, and there are no surplus funds available for "date nights," much less a vacation. They never seem to have fun anymore and both feel their lives are adrift. On top of everything, she has been feeling poorly; dizziness and nausea and sometimes severe chest pains come and go. She can't help but worry about that since her dad died of a heart attack.

Not surprisingly, Mark and Susan's marriage has been showing signs of strain. Their arguments center on two recurring themes, the first being time-prioritization. Mark feels Susan is not spending sufficient time with him or the children, and that the time he does get is when she's at her worst: tired and irritable. The second issue involves Mark's inability to get his career going again. His self-esteem is going downhill fast, and Susan feels he is being too selective and just needs to start working again in any professional capacity. Susan and Mark are beginning to feel that they jumped into marriage and children too quickly. Both have a nagging sense that what they're doing in life is not that important and certainly isn't utilizing their skills and abilities fully. Given the current level of mutual unhappiness, one might wonder:

1. What are the three major issues facing Susan and Mark?

2. For each major issue, what would you recommend they do?

As we think about Susan and Mark's situation, do you remember that assessment you took two chapters ago measuring stress in terms of forty-three "life events?" Did you notice that Susan had quite a few: death of a close family member, change in financial status, change in the frequency of marital disputes, change in work responsibilities, trouble with boss, change in work hours, change in eating habits, change in sleeping habits, personal illness, and possibly sexual difficulties. She also experienced several major changes in relationships: husband, daughters, boss, and mother.

By now you've probably come up with what you believe are the major issues or root causes of this couple's conflict: money, time for each other, children, Mom, Mark's faltering career, and Susan's poor health. And you probably had a lot of suggestions for Mark and Susan. You might have said that Mark has to get a full time job with benefits, even if it isn't in his chosen career field, or you may have recommended that while he is unemployed he shouldn't bother working part time as a carpenter, but instead should stay home with the children and save the day care costs. Or, you might ask, "How could he do that? He would never be able to go on job interviews, which is the long-term career solution."

You might say Susan must get a complete physical and start a nutritional program immediately . . . eating better, taking vitamin supplements, etc. Also, you might recommend that she give up her church work and Bible study until she has more time available. Or, you might say the opposite: don't give up the Bible study, because she is trying to get peace and harmony in her life and that may be a potential source of it. You might think she should visit her mom no more than once a week, since her Mom is already being taken care of, whereas her children need her more. Or, you might say that Susan should keep visiting her mom just as often as she does since, after all, it *is* her mother, and she might not be around much longer. Whatever your analysis and advice, chances are you saw this case objectively, rather than subjectively, because Susan and Mark aren't you. When we're detached from a situation, we can see things much more clearly than when we are intimately involved.

Seven-Dimensional Commitment Plan

Now let's go back to your personal assessment of the seven key life dimensions and build a personal commitment plan. A plan needs specific actions and deadlines. For each of the seven areas (especially those that you scored as contributing *most* to your stress), you need to create a series of actions that are either immediate (short term) or strategic (long term). Here are just some *examples* for each the seven dimensions:

A. **Family:**

1. Short term: Make a date night with your spouse to go to the movies or dinner.

2. Long Term: Engage in marital counseling or a marriage enrichment program together.

B. **Social:**

1. Short term: Resign from that volunteer board that is siphoning off all your spare time and accomplishing practically nothing.

2. Long Term: Use your newfound time to learn scuba diving (or whatever it is you commit to learn) and become certified, something you always dreamed of doing.

C. **Career:**

1. Short term: Schedule a meeting with your boss to better understand his or her perception of your current performance and career potential.

2. Long Term: Begin to explore other career opportunities or educational development programs to help aid your advancement.

D. **Spiritual:**

1. Short term: Begin an independent study on world religions, finding and reading some of the best books on the subject.

2. Long term: Join a Bible study to help you understand God's desire for your life, and become actively involved in a local church, synagogue, or other house of worship.

E. **Health:**

1. Short term: Eat breakfast, since all doctors and nutritionists think it's the most important meal of the day. Have only one cup of coffee in the morning, along with a healthy breakfast like oatmeal, seven-grain toast, or egg whites. Take the stairs at work or get up fifteen minutes earlier and walk around the block before your shower.

2. Long term: Set up a program with a nutritionist to create the right diet and additional supplements you need. Hire a personal trainer for a couple of months to help jump-start the right exercise program for you.

F. **Intellectual:**

1. Short term: Subscribe to and attend a lecture series at a local college or community center.

2. Long Term: Start the application process now (even if it's one course at a time) to get that degree you

have always wanted (associates, bachelors, masters, or Ph.D.).

G. Financial:

1. Short term: Create a weekly budget of actual income and expenses, and make a list of discretionary expense items that can be reduced.

2. Long Term: Enroll in a class to help you develop a comprehensive family financial plan for balanced investments and a way to become completely debt-free.

Personal Fulfillment Gap

Here's one more concept to work through. It may seem a little complicated, but bear with me; it's really not. Use figure 11 on the next page as a guide. First of all, think about the seven key dimensions of life and score each one of them as either being *extremely important* to your life at this time (5), *fairly important* (3), or *not important* to you right now (1). You realize that in different stages or phases of your life, priorities change. So, at an early age, your career may be critically important (5), and after retirement, less so (1). Health may be the opposite: less important when you're young, but more so when older. Now, after assessing all seven dimensions on their current degree of importance to you, enter the current level of joy, stress, or fulfillment (1–5) from your previous assessment work in Chapter Three. Finally, subtract the *current level of satisfaction* (B) from the *importance to you* (A) to determine the *fulfillment gap*.

For one dimension that is very important to you but also a key source of stress, the gap may be as large as four; for another

PERSONAL FULFILLMENT GAP

SEVEN KEY LIFE DIMENSIONS	A — IMPORTANCE TO YOU RIGHT NOW 5 = EXTREMELY 3 = FAIRLY 1 = NOT AT ALL	B CURRENT LEVEL OF FULFILLMENT & SATISFACTION 5 = GREAT 4 = GOOD 3 = NEUTRAL 2 = DISSATISFIED 1 = VERY DISSATISFIED	= C PERSONAL FULFILLMENT GAP
FAMILY			
SOCIAL			
CAREER			
SPIRITUAL			
HEALTH			
FINANCIAL			
INTELLECTUAL			

Figure 11

dimension that is not that important to you, the gap may be as low as zero, one, or even a negative score. Obviously you want to pour your personal energy into changing the areas of your life with the biggest gaps, those that are most important to you, and those in which you are not experiencing complete joy.

Now that you have some of your stress under control, we will begin the next leg of the journey with a *permanent* stress reliever: A personal life plan.

Section II

Getting Control of Your Life

Who Are You . . . and Why Are You Here?

CHAPTER FIVE

A PERSONAL LIFE PLAN: YOUR PERMANENT STRESS RELIEVER

"The life which is unexamined is not worth living."
—Plato

M an's search for meaning has been an enduring theme throughout time. From Socrates to Tolstoy, Twain to Thoreau, Simon and Garfunkel to Dave Matthews, philosophers, musicians, and artists across the centuries have explored man's need for fulfillment and for finding a sense of purpose in life—even in the most ordinary things.

The matter is as relevant today as it was in ancient times. According to a recent Barna Research Group poll, more than 40 percent of men and women are trying to figure out the meaning and purpose of their lives. It's a quest that cuts across all age groups, faiths, and ethnic heritages. We seem to be clear that life is a journey, but we don't know where we are going . . . or, frequently, why we're even taking the trip.

With so many still searching, why can't we figure it out? Are we more focused on making a living than on designing our lives? Are we so immersed in our jobs or our parenting that we are too busy to make time to think about why we are pursuing the path we are on? Has the frenzied pace of life kept us in a perpetual state of stress? Are we so snug in our comfort zone that we're afraid to chart a new course for our life? Have we reduced our expectations so much we've come to accept our current existence as "good enough"? Yet, do we have that nagging sense that defining a clearer life plan could turn our stress into strength, if only we had the time, tools, and motivation to get started?

A PERSONAL LIFE PLAN: YOUR PERMANENT STRESS RELIEVER

Whatever the reason, as we proceed down life's path, one truth begins to emerge very clearly: *If I don't control my destiny, someone else will—my parents, my spouse, my boss, my friends, or just circumstances . . . everyone and everything but me!* Rather than have someone else thrust destiny upon you, why not take control of your *own* life?

Each of us was created as a unique individual with the free will and reasoning to decide how to spend each of our years on earth. This is one of the core themes of this book. As the *Declaration of Independence* so eloquently put it, "All men are created equal . . . they are endowed by their Creator with certain inalienable rights . . . among these are life, liberty, and the pursuit of happiness."

The problem is that few of us are consciously pursuing the ideals set forth by America's founding fathers, and even fewer are realizing them, despite abundant evidence supporting the fact that those who take the time to examine their lives, understand their inner purpose, and chart a life plan become relatively happier, healthier, and wealthier.

It's often said that some people *let* things happen, some people *watch* things happen, and others *make* things happen. Which are you today, and which would you like to be tomorrow? The key to taking control of your life, making things happen, and finding your inner strength is simply this: having a *personal life plan.* What do I mean by "personal life plan"? First of all, I mean something that is explicit, not just

> Those who take the time to examine their lives, understand their inner purpose, and chart a life plan become relatively happier, healthier, and wealthier.

implied—a written document you can refer to regularly and modify and adapt as life's journey unfolds and you apply the wisdom gained through living each day. It is a tool for focusing your journey and reducing your stress.

In structure, think of your life plan as a pyramid. Your foundation is comprised of your unique values, your fundamental belief system, the principles or people for whom you'd give your life. This foundation is the area that requires the deepest introspection.

Once you fully understand your core values, the next level, built upon your values, is an articulation of your mission, your "raison d'être," your *reason for being*. Your *mission* is the basis for your *vision,* which resides on the next level. Your vision is a clear picture of where you'd like to be or what you'd like to be doing in your ideal future state. The next step is to turn that vision into specific *goals*. Goals are measurable, tangible, linear actions—the steps you'll take to achieve your dreams (more on all this later).

A PERSONAL LIFE PLAN

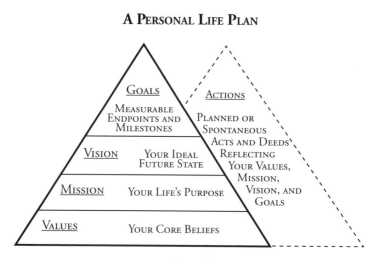

Figure 12

A PERSONAL LIFE PLAN: YOUR PERMANENT STRESS RELIEVER

Finally, as you complete your life plan, you'll develop *action plans*, which involve developing timetables for you to achieve your goals. Structured action plans provide support and hold you accountable to reach the goalposts that will get you where you want to go. Successful execution of the plan will achieve the goals that fulfill your vision according to your mission. And everything is based on your fundamental values. Now, that's a personal life plan!

A useful analogy is to think of your life as a business, with *you* as the CEO—the chief executive officer. For much of the twenty years I worked at IBM, I worked with highly acclaimed leadership experts and outstanding senior executives from a wide range of major corporations. One thing that became clear was that *all* successful and dynamic companies have core values or *basic beliefs*. These typically address the chief concerns of key stakeholders, such as customers, employees, or owners . . . and they incorporate such ideals as quality, excellence, service, innovation, and trust. As values get translated into common behaviors, they become a company's *culture*. And, of course, every great company has a sense of its own mission, based on its core competencies, which is usually something like, "providing the best products and services for our line of business."

At the next level, successful CEOs inspire a shared vision of where they plan to take their company over the next three to five years. They often push the process deeper into the organization by encouraging each business unit and department to have its *own* mission and vision statements, all aligned with the company's.

Geared toward making the vision a reality, they then have annual goals—clear, quantifiable objectives with timetables and many, many plans. One common aspect that relates to both the *business plan pyramid* and the *personal life plan pyramid* is that the elements at the bottom, the values and mission, have more permanency, while the goals and actions at the top are more dynamic or changeable. They are regularly revisited, "massaged," and updated in order to stay in tune with the ever-changing world around us.

If you work outside the home you're probably saying, "Of course my company has a mission, a vision, goals, and so on, and my department does, too, but what does that have to do with me?" Let me ask you this: Aren't *you* as important as your job? Shouldn't *your* life be as important as the life of your company? Well, certainly to you it is!

But, one question: "Will the work of creating a personal life plan be worth it in the end?" Yes! Here's just one example of how one man in counseling developed a new life plan that really changed his life.

A Case Study: David

David, a strong, handsome man in his 40s came to see me for career counseling. He was an editor at a major publishing house, but he just didn't feel fulfilled in his career. He was happily married and had two beautiful sons. The younger had Downs Syndrome.

David was a very optimistic man who loved his family and was very grateful to God for all he had been given. He loved his craft and desperately wanted to write fiction. Over the years he had begun many novels, but had never finished one.

After fewer than ten hours of consultation, David began to understand what was hindering his lifelong goal of publishing a book. His dual fears of *failure* and of *success*, with all that each would encompass, were paralyzing his writing efforts. After many, many hours of *thinking about* and then *writing out* his mission statement, and then harmonizing it with his spouse and job, he decided to leave his full-time job and work at home as an editor part time, and to write to completion his first novel. His wife supported his decision and took on the role of the family's major breadwinner for a time.

David's vision was simple: "I'm signing my books at Barnes and Noble Bookstore, and there are long lines of people waiting for me to sign the one they've just purchased." David worked up written goals that blocked out time segments when he would write. He planned *how* he would write, noting when he planned to accomplish each section and chapter. He asked two friends to be his "support partners" and hold him accountable to the established timelines. The three of them signed a contract that confirmed the dates they were to check in and see how he was doing and how often they would see what he had accomplished. David says the "support partners" were a critical part of the process.

I am happy to report that less than a year from the first day I met David, he had accomplished his lifelong dream. He says he couldn't have done it without the wrenching, deep-digging work he did creating his written mission statement.

Can you do the same? Absolutely! As psychologist and popular television personality Dr. Phil McGraw says, "You can't claim it if you can't name it." Name it, claim it, and you can do it! Remember, it's not the *intention* that counts. It's the *results*. Now, let's work our way up through the levels of the Life Plan Pyramid.

CHAPTER SIX

YOUR VALUES ARE UNIQUE

"What lies behind us and what lies before us are tiny matters compared to what lies within us."
—Oliver Wendell Holmes

Values constitute the often unexpressed, collective core beliefs that serve as an internal compass—a *conscience*—for our lives: honesty, compassion, freedom, happiness, respect, responsibility, tolerance, security, kindness, love, humility, and so on. Values comprise the essence of one's character. Every person has some combination of them, to different degrees and in widely varying proportions.

Some values are more accepted by society than others, and some are more accepted by an individual in the context of his or her private world. But, suffice it to say that *dissonance* between your core values and your daily actions or dissonance between your values and those around you can lead to stress. In contrast, *harmony* among your values, actions, and the values of those around you reinforces personal strength.

Sometimes you'll *say* you value something or someone, but your actions contradict the "espoused value." Quite simply, actions speak louder than words. Your credibility depends on the degree of consistency among three value dimensions: your real values, your espoused values (what you say you value), and your demonstrated values (what you actually do). For example, a husband or wife may articulate *family* as an important value, yet not be there when needed for Little League games or to help around the house. Does that spouse really value family? And do they think that by working long hours, arguably to support the family, they are demonstrating core values? Or is stating family as a priority just the "correct" thing to say? A peek at someone's calendar and checkbook will often yield a more accurate assessment of what their owner *really* values.

It's also important to understand the distinction between "means" values and "ends" values. Some things are valued because they are simply a means to an end. For example, money or family or "staying in shape" may be the means for different ends—power, security, acceptance, materialism, love, or health. So, family might get you love, money might get you power, staying fit might get you personal health, and so on.

People's values are good predictors of how they are likely to approach life. For example, if you value freedom, you may find it difficult to make a commitment that would limit your freedom. Values define your life purpose and shape your destiny. If your core belief system contains conflicting values, however, you're likely to sabotage anything you set out to do. To cite one example: If you want success, yet fear rejection, you're not going to get very far. If, on the other hand, freedom, power, and adventure are high on your values list, then security is probably at the bottom. In short, it's important to know what you value most.

Do you know what your core values are? Reflect long and hard on the following questions, and write your thoughts out in your personal journal or notebook:

- What's most important to me in life right now (family, money, success . . .)?

- What's most important to me in my career (challenge, ability to contribute, rewards . . .)?

- What's most important to me in relationships (passion, security, love, respect . . .)?

- What are the feelings I will do almost anything to avoid (anger, depression, embarrassment, disappointment . . .)?

If your values change, your destiny will change, as well. But before thinking about change, you have to understand where *your* unique values came from and define what they are today. Values can be an eclectic patchwork drawn from your own experience and that of others, as well as from parents, teachers, friends, and so forth. They become intrinsic to who you are through the experience of pain, pleasure, reward, and/or rejection. Sometimes you develop new values as you collect more life experiences. For example, if an ideal that you considered one of your core values ends up creating pain, you can deliberately abandon it and designate an appropriate successor. For example, you may value being on time to work and appointments. But suppose you are late to work because one of your children takes ill? You don't have to believe you are a less–than–dedicated employee. You can value punctuality and be a committed employee, yet also place a *higher* value on the health of your child. The values are not in conflict, but arranged according to your priorities.

Values can limit or liberate us. They can be the cage that confines us or the door we walk through to a more fulfilling life. You may believe that you are successful if you grow and learn and give to others. Or, you may believe success constitutes making ten million dollars a year. It depends on which of these things you value most.

> ## Values can limit or liberate us.

I'm sure some of you believe that you and your loved ones have the same values. Maybe that's true. But I'd also wager you and your loved ones interpret those values differently. *What does this mean?*

Consider this example: You and your spouse agree that you both value respect and believe it's very important that you show mutual respect. However, your spouse believes that part of respect is *never saying anything hurtful* to each other. If he gets angry, he will walk out of the room rather than raise his voice. You, on the other hand, believe that respect means *being totally open and telling each other everything,* even if it may be hurtful. If you are angry and raise your voice, you get over it. Your spouse, on the other hand, won't talk to you for days if you have raised your voice to him in disagreement. The essential truth here is that for a harmonious relationship, people need to understand each other's values and belief systems and work them out together. We may have the same values, but different ways of living them out.

So, our values are how we live as we pursue our mission and vision, and often our values don't get expressed until we craft a mission statement. Here's an example of a well–thought–out mission statement that explicitly incorporates someone's values. It's from contemporary author and motivational speaker Lee Milteer:

> "I live my life with perfect health, love, hap-
> piness, passion, creativity, flexibility—and give
> love to myself and others."

To create this, Milteer went through the mission–statement–development process we are about to discuss, but first she had to articulate and prioritize her values. She came up with: health, love, success, passion, spirituality, integrity, fun, adventure, honesty, intelligence, and harmony . . . and in that order.

In summary, our values serve as the foundation or *cornerstone* of our lives. If we can successfully build a personal mission statement based on those core values and then act accordingly, we can truly be fulfilled. Now, let's do just that!

CHAPTER SEVEN

DEVELOPING YOUR PERSONAL MISSION STATEMENT

"The man without a purpose is like a ship without a rudder—a waif, a nothing, a no man."
—Thomas Carlyle

A personal mission statement codifies the principle reasons you think you have been placed on this earth. It builds upon and amplifies the character strengths and values identified in your life plan, the qualities you have and want to develop, what you want to accomplish, and the values you want to live by. It is your *raison d'etre.* Management guru Peter Drucker says that, "Truly clarifying your purpose and [the] principles that elaborate your deepest beliefs is the hardest work you will ever do, but the most necessary to achieve what you desire."

A personal mission statement can be both confining and, at the same time, liberating. In her useful book, *The Path,* Laurie Beth Jones sees it as both a harness and a sword—harnessing you to what is true about your life and cutting away all that is false.

Viewed in another way, if you're not living your own personal mission statement, chances are you're living someone else's—a sure prescription for stress, not strength. Consider these common cases:

- A woman who, throughout her lifetime, was programmed by family, church, and friends to go to college to get two degrees, a B.S., and an *Mrs.,* then to work until she had 2.5 children to help save a little money for a down payment on a new home for the family. At that point, she was expected to give up her life to stay at home and tend to everyone else's needs. She never expected to be left feeling so unfulfilled when the kids grew up and left home, and she certainly never thought about what would become of her when her husband "fell out of love with her" and wanted a divorce.

- The '80s woman who thought she ought to have it all. After all, the song in the popular television commercial said she could "bring home the bacon and fry it up in a pan," and still be a dynamite lover for her man. She had a fabulous career; beautiful, healthy, happy children; and a supportive spouse—but learned that *doing it all* just didn't work, that something or someone had suffered.

- Or consider the man who always knew growing up that he'd go into his dad's business. There was no other choice for him, since he was the only child to carry on the family business. Or the fellow who grew up knowing he *had* to be an attorney or a doctor to make his hardworking parents proud that he was a "professional" man, the first in the long line of family that came over from the "old country." Or the guy that came from professional parents who expected him to work in a similar "white collar" field, yet all he wanted to do was work with his hands, outside, in an organic garden!

Sadly, too many of us let ourselves get saddled with someone else's mission for our lives, or just slip into a daily existence without ever dreaming of the possibilities beyond the "path of least resistance." How can you avoid this and discover what you were really born to do?

You may not yet know how to go about developing a mission statement. Perhaps it sounds like an overpowering task, and besides, when would you have time to work on it? This section will give you some tools to write out your mission statement. Then, if the possibility of living life to the fullest excites you, you'll *make* the time to work on it.

I promise it will be time well spent. Having a written mission statement helps you determine and focus your activities. It forces you to *dig deep* in thinking about your life and innermost feelings and the things in this world that really matter to you. Writing it down forces you to clarify and express your truest, most basic values and aspirations. It will brand your values and life purpose in your mind so they become a part of you instead of something you think about once and never again.

Making the Invisible Visible

Why is it so important to write down your mission, your goals, and your plans? Mark McCormack, in *What They Don't Teach You at Harvard Business School,* tells of a study conducted between 1979 and 1989. In 1979, graduates of the Harvard MBA program were asked, "Have you set clear, written goals for your future and made plans to accomplish them?" It turned out that only three percent of the graduates had written goals and plans. Thirteen percent had goals, but not in writing. Fully 84 percent had no specific goals at all.

Ten years later, in 1989, researchers interviewed the members of that same class again. They found that the 13 percent who'd had goals that were not in writing were earning twice as much as the 84 percent of students who had no goals at all. And most surprisingly, they found that the three percent of graduates who had clear, written goals when they left Harvard were earning, on average, *ten times as much* as the other 97 percent of graduates altogether. The only difference among the groups was the clarity of the goals they'd had for themselves when they graduated. Yes, you read that correctly. The three percent who'd had clear, written goals earned ten times as much as the 97 percent who didn't have clear, written goals. Almost all successful people have a mission and goals, and outstanding high achievers have a clearly defined written mission and goals.

Of course, economic gain isn't the only metric of success in life, but this study provides certainty that written commitments to yourself do, in fact, matter.

Developing your mission statement is neither easy, nor simple. It requires a deep look inward. It requires a serious evaluation of where you are in your life right now. It requires you to face reality *head on*. You

> Three percent of graduates who'd had clear, written goals when they left Harvard were earning, on average, ten times as much as the other 97 percent of graduates altogether.
> —Mark McCormack

may find yourself staring at things you don't want to see, at unpleasant facts about the way you've been living your life, but the potential benefits of developing a personal mission statement far outweigh the risks.

In committing your mission to paper, you will have to confess your innermost thoughts and feelings, if only to yourself. The good news is that your mission statement is *yours* alone. It is a clear, succinct, completely personal statement of your truest sense of life's meaning and your own purpose. However, when you've fleshed that out, you will undoubtedly want to harmonize what you've discovered about your personal mission with your career and, of course, with your most significant loved ones and other key people in your support structure.

Mission is also a spiritual concept. In fifty years of polling Americans, the Gallup organization has consistently found that 93% believe in God, 90% pray, 88% believe God loves them, and 33% report they've had a life-changing religious experience. So, it isn't surprising that many are searching for a sense of personal mission that is God-based.

Webster defines mission as "a continuing task or responsibility that one is destined, charged, or fitted to do." The two most-used synonyms are "calling" and "vocation." These concepts are represented by the same word in both English and Latin.

A vocation or calling, by nature, implies that *Someone* is doing the calling. Since a mission is "a calling," I personally agree with Richard Bolles, author of *What Color is Your Parachute,* that elements of our calling are from God, and so our mission could be:

1. To seek to know God and enjoy Him forever. If we go to God for guidance in this endeavor, He will grant what we wish for, if we come before Him and ask. After all, *He is calling us.*

2. To do what we can, every moment of every day, to make this world a better place, following the leading and guidance of God's Spirit within and around us.

   a. To fulfill our unique personal mission on earth.

   b. To exercise the talents we came to earth to use— our individual gifts.

   c. To do so in those settings that most appeal to us.

   d. To apply our gifts, blessings, and talents to address the needs and purposes that God seeks to fulfill in the world.

DEVELOPING YOUR PERSONAL MISSION STATEMENT

Those who don't believe in God or see their relationship to Him differently can, of course, still have a mission for their lives and create a written mission statement. It may be done without reference to God—defining a purpose *you* choose for your life, using the exercises here to identify your purpose and direction from a secular reference point.

To help frame your thinking, I've developed a series of questions for you to consider. They're not "multiple choice" and can't be answered with a simple *true* or *false*. You'll need several hours of quiet time to work through them, and it needn't be done all in one sitting. When you're ready to tackle them, try to go to a favorite getaway place—a beach, the mountains, somewhere far removed from your everyday life. Pick a place where you can stand apart from your habits and look at yourself in a way that enables you to take charge and create a bold plan for change. For me, that place has always been watching the ocean waves lap the sandy shore. They have been doing so over and over, again and again, for generations. How awesome the movement of the sea is compared to the minutiae of our lives that we make such a big deal about!

Take your journal with you, and write out your thoughts. Above all, be honest with yourself. Your thoughts are yours alone, unless you choose to share them. Please don't answer the questions as you would *like* to think or believe about them, but as you honestly do. If you're anything less than forthright in your responses, you'll be wasting your time. If you've heard about or have already done some of these exercises, don't skip them. It's always useful to see if your perspectives are still the same or are different now.

I urge you not to jump blindly into this. Read over the questions first, and take the time to prepare. Do some warm-up exercises. Try thinking your answers through during private moments—while stuck in traffic, cooking dinner, or languishing on "eternal hold" on the telephone.

Before exploring the "Twenty Big Questions," try these two exercises. The purpose is to get you to stretch your telescope, but use a wide-angle lens to *expand your perspective* actively and aggressively. Some of the questions may seem like downers and be difficult to answer, but reflecting on these things will be worth the effort, I promise you! And, please record your insights in your journal. No one will see it; no one will know what you've said but you. And once you have written your thoughts down, *you* will know yourself better, and that knowledge will be yours forever.

A. First Journaling Exercise

Imagine how you would feel if you were told you had just one year to live. What would be your first thought? Your first spoken response? Assuming you might do whatever you wanted with those months, with no economic or physical constraints, what would you want to do with your remaining time? What regrets would you have? Write it all out and then ask yourself: *Why am I not doing some of that now?*

B. Second Journaling Exercise

Plan your funeral. Let your imagination take you to your last farewell. Your body or ashes are resting peacefully while your friends and loved ones gather to celebrate your life. Who would be there? Do you believe you made an important difference in the lives of those attending? Who would speak at the service? What would they say? For what values and qualities of character will you be remembered? What contributions have you made that will be remembered? Perhaps more importantly, what will people say about you after the service is over? Did you make a real difference in anyone else's life? If you don't like your answers, perhaps you are not living with integrity. It's not too late!

DEVELOPING YOUR PERSONAL MISSION STATEMENT

The most moving funeral service I ever attended was not remarkable for its extravagance or flowery tributes. I sat in a small church listening intently to all different kinds of people reminiscing about a beloved friend, John, who had died at just thirty-three years of age. What struck me as most moving was that John always lived with integrity and courage, even during his final three-year fight with bone cancer. Everyone's life he touched, wherever he went, was forever changed.

C. Third Journaling Exercise

OK, it's time for your twenty questions. Go to that special place where it's completely quiet and you have no interruptions, even if you can only devote one hour at a time to this endeavor. This is not a test. It is simply a means of opening yourself up to thoughts and feelings you may not have known you had. The queries are designed to facilitate your introspection and help guide you toward a clear statement of your unique mission on earth, or life purpose.

1. What excites you the most? What most angers you? How can you use the first to affect or change the second?

2. What are the top three major decisions you have made that have had happy consequences in your life?

3. What is so important in your life that you'd be willing to die for it?

4. What qualities of character do you most admire in others?

5. Describe the people you know who seem to be the happiest. What common characteristics do they share?

6. Who are the three people in history you'd most like to have dinner with tonight? *Why?*

7. Who are the three people you think accomplished the most in their lifetimes?

8. What are the goals you have set for your life so far? Which have you accomplished?

9. If your resources were such that you did not have to work for a living, what would you do? *Why?*

10. What do you enjoy doing most when you have nothing to do?

11. Who is living the life you most envy? What do you think it is like?

12. What, in detail, is your ideal work setting? Your ideal work day? Your ideal coworker?

13. What would you like more of in your intimate relationships? *Less of?*

14. What would you do if you had more courage or were less risk-averse?

15. What have been your moments of greatest satisfaction? What do they have in common?

16. What do people who know you well think you're good at? What do they see as your greatest strengths?

17. What are the values you received from your family? Which have you accepted—and which rejected? Do you know why?

18. When you daydream, what kinds of great things do you see yourself doing?

19. When you put your work and personal life in perspective, what activities, respectively, are worth the most?

20. What are the things you do best that would be of the most value to others? Which of those things do you do now? If you were to do other things, which would they be?

Dealing honestly with all these questions is probably pretty overwhelming. In all likelihood, you have put things down that you have sort of *thought* about from time to time but never actually articulated. You may also have surfaced things you never truly admitted to yourself before.

Your next step is to incorporate what you have learned about yourself into your *mission statement*. Whatever its format, a good mission statement has three basic attributes:

1. It is no more than a single sentence long (approximately 13–16 words).

2. It's easy to understand.

3. It's easy to commit to memory.

From the journal entries you've made thus far, summarize your conclusions:

What you'd like to be:

_____

_____

What you'd like to do:

_____

_____

The values you choose to live by:

_____

_____

To crystallize your mission and keep it short requires being extremely precise, picking just the right words. A *mission* requires action, and verbs are action words. Pick three verbs that you think are the most meaningful, purposeful, and exciting for you. Here are a few suggestions:

> *accomplish, acquire, advance, affect, affirm, alleviate, communicate, compel, create, demonstrate, distribute, drive, enable, educate, embrace, engage, engineer, foster, facilitate, launch, lead, measure, model, motivate, nurture, persuade, produce, progress, promote, reform, restore, safeguard, serve, stand, sustain, touch, utilize, validate, venture, volunteer, yield.*

Now do the same for the value(s) or purpose(s) to which you would devote your life. What are you really passionate about? Choices here might include such things as:

justice, family, freedom, service, excellence, equality, creativity, etc.

Next, who, and what, are you here to help?

The environment, health care, children, the poor, agricultural practices, law and order, politics, government, the animals, civil rights, disabled persons, women, men, third-world countries, the incarcerated, mankind, families, medical research, etc.

Put those three pieces together, and you have a mission statement that might read like this:

My mission is to _____, _____, and

_____ (your three verbs)

_____ (your core values) to, for or with

_____ (group/cause that excites you).

This format is hardly set in stone. It's merely an example, meant to provide some guidance as you set out to write your own. Please don't be put in a box about this mission statement. It's yours and yours alone. Do whatever works for you!

My own personal mission statement is: "To use my God-given gifts of leadership, teaching, counseling, and compassion to enable others to be empowered to thrive through life's transitions."

Here's a sampling of both career and personal mission statements from others:

Paula Van Ness—CEO and President of "Make a Wish Foundation"

The company *mission* is: "To create moments of hope, strength, laughter, and dignity that improve the lives of our wish children, regardless of their medical condition."

The *vision* is that "One day, everyone walking this earth will experience the life-affirming, life-altering, addictive, and exquisitely blessed power of a wish."

Lt. General Dave R. Palmer, Superintendent, United States Military Academy at West Point (1986–1991): "To develop leaders of character to provide for the common defense of the nation."

Hopeline Women's Center, Connecticut: "Hopeline promotes the sanctity of human life by providing education and Christ-centered counseling, guidance, and support for anyone seeking help with pregnancy-related issues."

Bernie Siegel, cancer surgeon, author, and speaker: "I am a surgeon who writes books and gives seminars to teach people what I have learned, and I'm still learning how to deal with life's difficulties."

IBM Corporation, 2002: "To be the world's most successful and important information technology company . . . successful in helping our customers apply technology to solve their problems, and successful in introducing this extraordinary technology to new customers."

Don Winkler, CEO of Ford Motor Credit. Winkler, who has severe dyslexia, has a *visual* mission statement: A rocket ship represents the goal of developing products with speed and simplicity. The driver has a telescope to maintain the vision. The crowds of people are potential workers passing through a funnel, representing Ford's desire to recruit the best. Handshakes show that Ford Credit must work with partners, such as Ford dealerships.

Abraham Lincoln's stated mission was, "to preserve the Union." **FDR's** was, "to end The Depression." **Nelson Mandela's** was, "to end Apartheid." **Mother Theresa's** was, "to show mercy and compassion to the dying." **Joan of Arc's** was, "to free France from oppression." The biblical Nehemiah's was, "to rebuild the walls of Jerusalem." Moses' mission was, "to free the Israelites from slavery in Egypt and deliver them to the Promised Land."

After studying the book of Acts, I believe the mission statement of the **Apostle Paul** would read something like this: "My mission is, with the enabling power of the Holy Spirit, to reach every person on earth with the good news of Jesus Christ and to plant a church in every major city throughout the world."

Here are a few others:

- **Manager:** "To foster innovation, enhance cooperation, and create prosperity for everyone I serve."

- **Nurse:** "Out of the rich reservoir of love that God seems to have given me, to nurture and show love to others, most particularly to those who are suffering from incurable diseases."

- **Bible Teacher:** "To draw maps for people to show them how to get to God."

- **Organic farmer:** "To create the purest foods I can, to help people's bodies not get in the way of their spiritual growth."

- **Gardener:** "To create beautiful gardens so that in the lilies of the field, people may behold the beauty of God and be reminded of the beauty of holiness."

- **Comedian/motivational speaker:** "My mission is to make people laugh so that the travail of this earthly life doesn't seem quite so hard to them."

- **Reporter:** "To help people know the truth, in love, about what is happening out in the world, so that there will be more honesty in the world."

- **Hospice worker:** "My mission is to weep with those who weep, so that in my arms they may feel themselves in the arms of that Eternal Love that sent me and that created them."

Each of the above is a beautiful mission statement and, as such, a good start for its creator. Taking it to the next level requires incorporating how the owner of the statement will fulfill the stated mission and how it impacts his or her role *vis-à-vis* surrounding individuals.

Here's a particularly good example of a senior executive's full-loop mission, from Steven Covey's *The Seven Habits of Highly Effective People:*

"My mission is to live with integrity and to make a difference in the lives of others."

To fulfill this mission:

- I have charity: I seek out and love the one, each one, regardless of his/her situation.

- I sacrifice: I devote my time, talents, and resources to my mission.

- I inspire: I teach by example that we are all children of a loving Heavenly Father, and that every Goliath can be overcome.

- I am practical: What I do makes a difference in the lives of others.

These roles take priority in achieving my mission:

- Husband: My partner is the most important person in my life.

- Together we contribute the fruits of harmony, industry, charity, and thrift.

- Father: I help my children experience progressively greater joy in their lives.

- Son/brother: I am frequently "there" for support and love.

- Christian: God can count on me to keep my covenants and to serve His other children.

- Neighbor: The love of Christ is visible through my actions toward others.

- Change Agent: I am a catalyst for developing high performance in large organizations.

- Scholar: I learn important new things every day.

As you can see, the sixteen words of the mission statement wouldn't mean a great deal if the executive hadn't followed them up with *how* he would fulfill his mission and the roles that would take priority in his doing so.

Once you have a written mission statement, it's imperative to align it with your life partner and with your career. For example, if your personal mission were to live as a housemother in a home for unwed mothers in New York City, and your partner wanted to be a cattle rancher in Montana, you two would have your work cut out for you! Or, if you had a passion and a mission for helping disadvantaged youth, but you worked as a day trader on Wall Street, you might have a different but equally major conflict to resolve. You wouldn't necessarily have to give up your day job if it was satisfying to you in ways beyond monetary increase; you could still follow your passion as an *avocation*, doing volunteer work with disadvantaged youth, for instance.

I've offered these examples simply to help frame your thinking throughout this process. If they give you ideas, *great*, but please don't let any unduly influence your own mission statement, which should arise from the passion of your own heart and soul.

When you have completed your *draft mission statement,* carry it with you for awhile and adjust it as much as you wish—add and delete, make notes, keep thinking about what you've said. After a bit, have another go at it. It may take several rewrites before you feel satisfied with the results. After you complete your mission statement, evaluate it carefully, and remember that as you change and grow, your perspective and values may undergo some change, as well.

Don't let your statement become outdated. Periodic review and evaluation is helpful in keeping you in touch with your own personal development.

Some of you may take your time with this for awhile. Some may even answer all of the questions . . . until it comes to the writing of the mission statement, then quit. I encourage you to write out a personal mission statement in whatever format fits your style. But the most important piece is to *live* this personal mission. In doing so, you'll see that everything you do, everything that happens, every decision you make, will be guided by your mission. Once you've defined your mission, you will ask yourself constantly, "Is this aligned with my mission?" or "How does this harmonize with the way I have chosen to live my life?" Your mission will guide every decision you then make.

So, now you have a sense of your mission, your core purpose—and a written mission statement you can begin to use as a touchstone as life proceeds. If you've gotten this far, you should be very proud of yourself! It was a great deal of hard work. Of course, you're not done yet. Now let's look at where you might see yourself in three-to-five years in relationship to your mission.

CHAPTER EIGHT

ENVISIONING AN IDEAL FUTURE STATE

*"Dreams are renewable no matter what our age or condition;
there are still untapped possibilities within us and new beauty
waiting to be born."*

—Dr. Dale Turner

There are many definitions of the word *vision*, but my favorite is from *The Leadership Challenge,* by James Kouzes and Barry Posner. "A vision is an ideal and unique image of the future," the authors state. I find that being able to see that future, ideal state in your mind's eye gives you comfort, hope, and a sense of purpose. Without it, you are buffeted about by the winds of daily chaos, and dealing with that state of uncertainty is a root cause of stress.

A vision is a statement that describes the destination we hope to reach at the end of all our labors. It is future-oriented. If we don't know what our future destination should look like, we can't begin to get there. Your personal vision will engage your heart and spirit. It's a simple and *living* document. It's compelling, and it expresses hope. It's a possibility, not a probability. It's a quantum leap, and it's motivational.

Your *vision statement* defines your desired future state—the deepest expression of how you want your emerging reality to manifest itself. It describes how you want your life to be and how you seek to create that life for yourself. It must appeal to your physical senses, your emotional needs, and your spiritual quest. It's not just a probability but a possibility, an expanded statement of your mission. Visions are essential, because without a vision, we sometimes look at what's not working rather than at what might work better. Significant vision precedes significant success. Every architect "sees" the building before he or she begins the design. Your vision—what you see before you begin to build—is what spurs you on to live out your mission. If you can see it, you can make it happen in time. If you can't see it, you never will.

My brother-in-law, Tom, was very bright—a "whole-brain thinker," both mechanical and artistic . . . very active, but with a restless spirit. Frankly, he was a little rebellious. As an adolescent, his interests varied widely . . . from sports, to leading his own dance band, to rebuilding cars in his parents' garage. While his parents (my in-laws) wanted him to pursue his education above all else, he had other ideas, and he decided to leave high school, join the Air Force, and see the world. It was in the Air Force that his mechanical and engineering instincts were awakened. He began to envision a future in which he was designing advanced aircraft, like the airplanes he was flying . . . very hard to do without a high school diploma! But, with his vision sharpening, he decided to make the effort to finish high school, then enroll in college, and eventually earn his bachelor's degree in aeronautical engineering.

After the Air Force experience, he joined the United Technology Corporation's research team, testing advanced aircraft and engines in their giant wind tunnels. But, he soon realized that his initial vision of designing aircraft was less satisfying and exciting than creating new technology businesses. So, after securing an MBA, he joined UTC's Corporate Strategy Team, leading new venture exploration. Unfortunately, little real venturing happens inside large corporations, so he left UTC and formed a new venture capital firm with a few other senior executives. They created a portfolio of nearly one hundred new technology startups. He ended up becoming the CEO of one of the most successful robotic businesses, one that helped revolutionize hospitals and the medical industry.

So, while a vision of your future can help motivate action, can change and can progress, it doesn't *have* to remain static. It can certainly be modified over time as new learning and insights arrive. In Tom's case, by envisioning a more ideal future state and pursuing it with determined action, he found ways to fully use his God-given skills and talents.

Researching Your Vision

As society becomes increasingly technological and ever-more connected through the Internet, envisioning can now become more efficient and visual. Research can be more self-driven than ever. If you use the Internet, try "googling" some of the ideas you have, then explore new careers, classes in subject areas of new interest, and find experts in your area who are already pursuing part of your dream. Contact them online for more information. If they have a web page, many professionals welcome the opportunity to discuss what they do, talk about their experiences, and give you a chance to validate or refine your vision. Who knows? You might discover a new coach to help guide you in your decision processes.

Vision Exercise

Let's try something. Put on the kind of relaxing music you might hear in the background when you're getting a massage, and settle yourself into a comfortable chair. Close your eyes and breathe deeply. Relax. Let your mind relax. Let your head relax, then your arms, chest, and stomach. Keep breathing. Now relax your fingers, your legs, and your toes. Keep breathing, nice and deeply.

Next, if you aren't asleep by now, try *envisioning* some part of the mission you've outlined. You have your mission statement written out. Now, what will your future look like if you live out your mission? Imagine it is five years from now, and it's 9 A.M.

on a Monday morning. Where are you? What are you doing? Who are you seeing? What are you wearing? Now it's noon; same questions. Now it's Saturday; same questions.

Your hometown newspaper or a national magazine is writing an article about you. What's it about? What have you done that's changed the community or your business, and how? Maybe the article was prompted by an award you've just received. What did you win the award for?

When you open your eyes, write down some of the things you've just envisioned. Are they real possibilities? Some, at least, probably are.

Now take all this information and, in twenty-five words or less, use it to write out your ideal and unique image of the future. It needs to be short so you can remember it and share it in order to inspire others. Once you've written it out, you may want to draw it, as well. If you are as bad of an artist as I am, you might decide to find some kind of picture that resembles it. You may even want to have a short phrase or slogan that would be useful for communicating your vision to others. Consider the General Electric Company's slogan: "We bring good things to life." It's brilliant because it's succinct, forward-looking, graphic, and right on point.

Here is a sampling of more effective business and personal vision statements:

Apple Computer (whose vision has never really changed since its founding in 1977): "By putting powerful technology that was once available only to a few in the hands of as many people as possible, we can transform the way people think, learn, and communicate."

IBM, in 2002: "IBM will continue to be the basic resource of much of what is invented in our industry."

Ulysses S. Grant's vision for his presidency: "For the United States to become a nation of great power and intelligence, with peace, happiness, and prosperity at home, and the respect of other nations."

Christopher Columbus: To return to Spain with ships full of spices, converts, and gold. (It was this vision that inspired Queen Isabella to give him the money for the journey. If he had just gone to her and asked for money, men, ships, and plenty of time, she might not have granted him the substantial funds required.)

Jane Logan (pseudonym): one of the first black women colonels in the army. When she was picking cotton as a teenager in Alabama, she envisioned that someday she would be in a leadership position in the armed forces and be able to mentor other black women. (I met her on an airplane on her way to give a speech at the Pentagon about the creation of a mentoring program for minority women in the army.)

Victor Frankel, the philosopher-psychiatrist author of *Man's Search for Meaning,* had a great deal to say about having a vision. He has said that when he was in a Nazi concentration camp he had three goals: to survive, to help others, and to try and learn something. He accomplished all three. On the learning front, he found it wasn't always the young and strong who survived. He believed the common thread among those who did was having, "something significant yet to do in their future." Frankel knew he needed to write a book about the camps, and every day he saw himself at some future date giving motivational speeches based on his experiences to large groups of people. He believed that vision is what spurred him on when others gave up.

In *How to Argue and Win Every Time,* author and trial lawyer Gerry Spence writes that in gaining a victory for one of his clients he told the jury: "After your deliberations, I want all of us to walk out of this courtroom as free people. I want to walk out as a free person. I want you to walk out as a free person, and I want my client to walk out as a free person, knowing justice has been done." He related that after the jury did free his client, one of the jurors came up to him and thanked him for being so direct with what he'd said. That was what they wanted also, and Gerry's words made it all come together for them. If he had just said, "I want you to find my client *not guilty*," there wouldn't have been a powerful vision of freedom in their minds.

The old proverb: "Where there is no vision, the people perish," still holds true today (Proverbs 29:18). There is a common metaphor of a rope crossing a river with rapids. You cross that river hanging on to that rope to get to the other side. No matter how difficult it is to stay clear of the rapids, you cling to that rope. The rope is your *mission,* and it helps hold you up, but it's the sight of the land on the far shore of the river that keeps you going. That's your *vision.* Our values are how we will live as we pursue our mission and vision. Our *values* are the way we measure the rightness of our direction.

Futurist Joel Barker tells a story about an old man who was very unhappy with how his life had progressed. He couldn't see that he had accomplished anything of any importance at all. He was sitting on the beach one day, feeling extremely depressed, when he saw a young man walking in the hot sun, picking up the starfish that had been washed ashore with the tide, and throwing them back into the ocean.

The old man spoke.

"Son, don't you see that what you're doing makes no difference? You'll never be able to throw most of them back in the ocean before they burn up."

The young man looked at the elder and, with a starfish in his hand, ran toward the foaming surf. As he thrust his arm back to hurl it into the water, he said, "It makes a difference for this one!"

Sometimes we feel like just another starfish on the vast shoreline of life, and sometimes we feel like the old man. We think we haven't accomplished what we'd hoped we would. But, I urge you to keep in mind that it is *never too late* to feel like the younger man, and to proclaim that nothing is a waste of time if we are able to use our God-given gifts and acquired skills to help one person . . . one starfish . . . at a time.

> Action without vision is passing the time. Vision without action is merely a dream. But action with vision can change the world.

What's your vision?

CHAPTER NINE

GOALS ARE DREAMS WITH DEADLINES

*"When we are motivated by goals that have deep meaning,
by dreams that need completion, by pure love that needs
expressing, then we truly live life."*

—Greg Anderson

Now that you have uncovered your *core values*, written your *mission statement* (sense of purpose), and dreamed your *vision statement* (your future, ideal state), it's time to set goals that will support the fulfillment of your mission and guide you towards the creation of your vision. Goals are measurable, rational, tangible, linear actions—the small steps toward achieving your dreams. Clarity of goals enables the creation of clear, quantifiable milestones and *focus*, which builds strength. The absence of goals or "yardsticks for assessing progress" contributes to uncertainty, self-doubt, and *stress*.

Goals should engage your spirit and lift you up to new heights, allowing you to overcome self-imposed limitations and personal failings. Goals, in essence, are *dreams with deadlines*. They create the future in advance. I would suggest you set goals for the seven key dimensions of life, which usually coincide with the important roles you identified in your mission statement. Recall, the seven key dimensions are:

- **Family**
- **Social**
- **Career**
- **Spiritual**

- **Physical**
- **Intellectual**
- **Financial.**

Check the senior executive's mission statement in Chapter Six to see how his different roles meshed with his life's seven key dimensions. For our executive, it looked like this:

- **Family**   = Father, Husband, Son, Brother
- **Social**   = Neighbor
- **Spiritual**   = Christian
- **Career**   = Change-agent
- **Intellectual** = Scholar

Since **physical** (taking care of one's health) and **financial** (taking care of one's money) are two of the seven areas of life, but are not "roles" one plays, this executive didn't include them in his mission. That doesn't mean they can't be in *yours*, however.

The goals you make in each of these areas should be written, in order to make them clear. They also need to have *checkpoints* and *deadlines*. They need to be specific, measurable, and realistic. Get excited about your goal-setting! You don't need to reinvent the wheel. Draw from other people's ideas and successful techniques, adjusting them to fit your style and personality. Cut out pictures that have to do with your goals and put them on poster board, where you'll see them every day. Many athletes do that when they are training for a marathon or an Olympic event. If they *see* it, they can *believe* it—and that's a big part of what it takes to make it happen.

When I first became a manager at IBM, the company sent me to first-line management school, along with all the other new first-line managers, to learn what it takes to be a successful manager. After only a few days at the school, I knew that within three-to-five years I wanted to be an instructor there. Foremost among the requirements for an instructor's post was having excellence in one's own management skills. The second was to be a good speaker and motivator, in order to help new managers learn those skills.

With that vision in mind, my mission was to use my skills of coaching, counseling, and empathy, along with knowledge of the business, to bring dramatic improvement to the department I had just inherited. I'd been handed the department that had the worst "opinion survey results" in the division. I was bent on making it the best department at IBM in about a year's time, while at the same time achieving all the organization's business goals. I could only do that by using my values, my skills, and my experience to create an environment that would motivate people to higher achievement.

Leaders can't lead alone. They need to have a vision, and they have to inspire others to believe in their vision. They have to enable others to reach *their* goals and develop their people as a team. People need praise and encouragement along the way. As the head of the department, I knew that I had to live with integrity every single day, in every single instance, in order to gain my team's trust.

If you recall my present mission statement, stated in Chapter Seven, you'll see that it's very similar to the one I had back in 1982. Although I no longer work at a major corporation, and I'm certainly in a different career, in a different season in my life, I'm still using the gifts and abilities I have for the facilitation and growth of others, so my mission hasn't changed entirely.

My vision back then was to be teaching in the IBM Management Development School. I could see myself very clearly doing that job, up there in the front of the room sharing my "war stories" and all the necessary information these brand new, first-line managers needed to know to help their people become the best that they could be. I knew I had to be an excellent first-line manager myself—and an excellent middle manager, as well.

A few promotions came my way during that period. I worked exceptionally hard and enjoyed the process of learning to manage departments, but I always focused on teaching in IBM's Management Development School within three–to–five years. Meanwhile, I developed and presented many topics for employee training meetings, including the cultivation of positive attitudes, stress management, and conflict resolution. Of course, I developed all of these on my own time, not the company's. Colleagues occasionally asked why I wanted to do so much work when I wasn't getting paid for it. My answer was that I knew it would help develop me and my presentation skills, as well as help the students in the class to be better employees.

The point here is that I had developed written goals that I accomplished, step by step, in reaching toward my vision. Yes, and within three years I was teaching at IBM's Management Development School—helping both new and experienced managers to achieve *their* missions! And that led to more opportunity. Later in my career, I found myself there again, developing the company's *Transformational Leadership* curriculum for the 90s at the newly expanded "IBM Leadership Center."

Remember this: A *purpose* will almost always be stronger than an outcome. What your goals *make of you* as a person is much more important than whatever you'll achieve by setting them (though you will definitely achieve more *with* than *without* clearly defined goals). The reason most people make resolutions on New Year's Eve but rarely follow through with them is because they don't understand the power of consistent goal-setting. They don't go about creating—and *refining*—goals that really matter to them. They don't know the answer to the real question: "Why? Why must I achieve this goal at this time?"

Having a vision of the end product—a fulfilled mission—tells you why.

You've often heard it said that the first step to recovery, in anything, is the diagnosis. In this process, *reason* is the diagnosis. Reason comes first; answers follow. If you have a *why*, you'll figure out a *how*. Be persistent. It is the key to successful goal achievement. Don't allow yourself to become distracted with excuses for why things can't be done. Excuses are the enemies of goal achievement. And nothing takes the place of persistence. Nothing is more common than unsuccessful people with talent, and the world is full of educated people who are very unsuccessful. Persistence and determination about your mission, your vision, and your goals enables you to achieve them.

Goal-Setting Questions

Let's look again at the seven dimensions of your life, and let me offer some thought-provoking questions to help you start setting your own goals.

Family

♦ How can you improve how you express your love to your spouse?

♦ What can you do to create a closer relationship with family members?

♦ How can you be a better role model to your children? Give specifics.

♦ What family activities could you get started to improve everyone's relationships?

♦ If your calendar shows where you spend your time, how much is written in for your family?

◆ What changes can you make to ensure that you spend more quality time with the people you say are most important in your life?

Social

◆ What volunteer activities interest you? Will you pursue giving some time to one? If so, how much?

◆ When can you schedule fun time for yourself, perhaps with old friends? How can you make new friends?

◆ Where do you want to vacation, and how can you plan for it?

Career

◆ Are you really happy doing what you are doing? If not, what do you want to do, and how can you get there?

◆ How can you keep a positive attitude (i.e., "fly with the eagles") when the turkeys get you down?

◆ What can you do to increase your skill base . . . or any other education you need?

◆ How can you improve your level of enjoyment for your work?

Spiritual

◆ What books can you read, including the Bible, to get more in touch with your spiritual side?

◆ How much time can you spend in prayer or meditation each day?

- What houses of worship can you attend? Will you make a commitment to do so regularly?

- How can you begin to forgive those who have wronged you?

- How can you release your guilt, anger, envy, or hostile feelings toward others?

Physical

- What can you do in the next year to become healthier and in better shape?

- What type of workout can you do, and how often? Where can you do it?

- What support system can you put in place to help keep you focused and on-target?

- Is there a particular sport you once wanted to learn that you can take up now?

- What type of foods can you add to your diet to nurture your body?

- What harmful foods can you eliminate?

Intellectual

- What and how many nonfiction books are you planning to read this year?

- Are you thinking about going back to school?

- What decisions need to be made to consider your returning to school?

- What new skills are you planning to learn?

Financial

- How much are you saving this year?

- How much is for retirement?

- What type of investments will you make this year?

- How much are you budgeting for your education fund? Your children's education fund?

Action to Character to Destiny

There is no question that this process involves a lot of work, but it should. After all, you are trying to achieve your destiny, to "be all you can be," as the U.S. Army slogan goes. We each have one life—and usually only a few chances at reaching our highest destiny. The last critical step in getting control of your life is to translate into action the values, mission, vision, and goals you've worked so hard to discern and articulate. No one summed it up better than William Makepeace Thackeray, who wrote:

> "Sow a thought, reap an action,
>   Sow an action, reap a habit,
>   Sow a set of habits, reap a character,
>   Sow a character, reap a destiny."

It is *our* thoughts that ultimately dictate our approach to life, our reactions and responses to daily events. And, as you will see in the next section, getting control of your mind and thoughts can significantly enable your progress and contentment, and failure to do so can significantly hinder them. Translating your thoughts into actions by *walking the talk* demonstrates your inner values externally, and repeating new actions develops them into habits. Good habits can result in good character, the all-important ingredient of personal leadership, good friendship, and human trust. Our *reputation* is how others perceive us externally, but our *character* is internal. The contrasts between the two are dramatic:

- The circumstances in which you live may determine your reputation; the truths you live determine your character.

- Reputation covers the outside; character grows from within, like an oak . . . slow and strong.

- Your reputation can be earned in an hour; your character is built in a lifetime.

- Reputation is what men write on your tombstone; character is what God knows is in your heart.

Each of us aspires to be authentic. It is best when reputation and character are in sync, when what you say you believe, what you really believe, and what you do are all in alignment.

As we work towards developing character and destiny, some actions can be preplanned. For example, your life plan may require that you schedule more time with your family and friends, enroll in an education course to improve your mind or career, or invest your time to further your spiritual, intellectual, or financial growth. Of course, as you commit to these transforming actions, you need to set specific timeframes and deadlines to achieve your goals and reach your destiny.

The *more* challenging thing is to live your life each day according to your newly clarified values, mission, and vision. This means dropping some deep-seated habits and developing new ones. It isn't always easy. You may want to find someone to support you during this change process and to hold you accountable for your actions. Why not choose one or two close friends whom you respect and know will confront you both honestly and lovingly about fulfilling these commitments to yourself?

Taking control of your life is really about realizing that you *can* control your destiny and that *the present* is the time to take action on it. William Jennings Bryan said: "Destiny is not a matter of chance; it is a matter of choice. It is not a thing to be waited for; it is a thing to be achieved."

So, where do you begin? It starts with taking control of your mind as a personal decision that leads to actions and habits that ultimately grow into character and destiny. Read on, and discover how to do just that!

SECTION III

Getting Control Of Your Mind

A Roadmap to Healthier Behavior

CHAPTER TEN

STOP COMPLAINING AND DEAL WITH IT!

"What upsets people are not things themselves, but their judgments about the things."
—Epictetus, A.D. 50–130

Developing a life plan is a monumental step towards personal transformation. The next challenge is to actually implement the actions called for, which may involve changing our behavior in significant ways—*no simple task!* It requires that we begin to understand, then dramatically adjust, our mind-sets or *mental models.*

Many times in life we know exactly what we *should* do, but a variety of obstacles derail us and keep us from accomplishing it. In this section we will examine some of the mental traps that send us reeling off the tracks, and introduce a process for you to get control of your mind and help you reach the destination defined in your life plan.

When I worked as a counselor, I found the very first session was usually the most critical. It was at the outset that the client and I developed both goals for therapy and the expectations of the counselor. I needed a commitment that the client was willing to really *work* for the changes desired, and I used homework, reading assignments, and personality assessments to help reinforce the new "way of being" he or she desired. It was by no means a passive experience, but an active one in which I provided the tools, and the client worked at whatever transformation was needed. The same applies here in this self-guided approach. You can't expect change unless you're committed to work at something new.

In my office I had a magic wand over my desk to remind clients I couldn't wave that wand and make their lives better. All I could do was give them the tools and support to help make that happen. A typical series of counseling sessions ran approximately six to eight weeks, as we challenged the client's rigid "musts, shoulds, and demands" that were internalized from his or her values, not the inherent or learned values themselves. Were there "thinking errors" blinding them to possible solutions to their painful problems? Very often there were. Consider, for example, these three situations:

> Janice has given unconditional love to the stepdaughter she's helped raise since the age of twelve. Though the daughter is now in her thirties, Janet feels no love or respect has ever been returned to her. Because she believes that for all she has given up and done for this child she should be shown respect and love, she feels justified in her anger.
>
> She sees that her friends, whom she believes haven't been nearly as good as stepmothers, are practically *worshipped* by their stepchildren. She feels sorry for herself as she relives in her mind the ingratitude expressed towards her every day by this child. In fact, the more she thinks about it, the angrier she gets—and the angrier she gets, the more inflamed her ulcer gets. . . .

> Joe's son, Joey, Jr., throws the door open and heads directly for his bedroom. Out of the

corner of his eye, Dad notices his shirt is torn and, once again, that his son is in tears. "I haven't eaten," he shouts, "because somebody took my lunch money!"

Joey, Jr., has been picked on in school by bullies since he was in fifth grade. He is now in junior high, and it seems to be getting worse. Joe senior was, himself, always a small, weak kid growing up and is now pained to see his son going through this same thing. He has talked to the school about this, but to no avail.

It seems there are no consequences to these bad kids' behaviors. He is having awful feelings about these hoodlums picking on his son. He is so angry with these "evil kids" that he sometimes takes it out on his wife, saying she is making Joey, Jr., into a sissy . . . and sometimes he gets very angry with his son for not sticking up for himself. . . .

Lauren has been working for a major corporation for fifteen years. She started at the bottom and worked her way up the corporate ladder. She was promoted into management and loved her job, handling the "people management" part of the job extremely well. However, her new manager is extremely difficult. It seems that nothing pleases her. No matter what she does, it's not good enough. There is obviously a personality conflict between them.

Lauren has tried to talk to her manager about this, but to no avail. She can't go to her second-line manager about it, because he is a very good personal friend of her boss. She is so stressed about this situation, she can think of nothing else. She believes her job is in jeopardy. She complains to everyone she knows, all the time, and can't sleep at night. She is a single Mom, and she needs this job for the medical benefits, or she would leave before she's let go.

The above scenarios illustrate modern dilemmas, some of which may relate to your own experiences. Although the circumstances of each are very different, they share a common dimension in that the natural response to each episode and the emotions each person felt are based on some deeply ingrained mental models. They are learned habitual responses, in some cases valid and rational, and in others completely invalid and irrational, that dramatically affected behavior. As we begin to address this, I believe the theory and approach outlined below can be truly valuable for everyone.

"As a Man Thinks, So Is He" (Proverbs 23:7)

Many times in life we know exactly what we *should* do, but a variety of mental inhibitors derail us along the way and keep us from doing it. In this section we will examine some common "mental traps" and introduce a simple method for getting control of your mind so that you can accomplish your life plan.

The field of psychology is filled with literally hundreds of personality and behavioral theories. Some therapies are based on getting insight into one's past, asserting this is sufficient to start the change process. Other therapies focus on getting clients in touch with their feelings. One of the most practical and successful in helping people deal with personal and family problems is called Rational Emotive Behavior Therapy (REBT, or RET). It's based on the premise that people *distress themselves* emotionally when they take their acquired beliefs and irrationally reconstruct them into absolute, rigid demands on both themselves and others. REBT helps people develop a philosophy of *flexibility* and *acceptance* that can really help improve interpersonal, marriage, and family relationships. This means *accepting human fallibility* and accepting responsibility for one's own behavior. The resulting benefits can be unconditional acceptance of self and others.

REBT is the lifelong contribution of psychologist Albert Ellis, who was born in 1913 and died ninety-five years later, in 2007. He practiced at his Manhattan Institute, until 2005. I had the distinct pleasure of meeting him when I was in graduate school. Every Friday night for decades, he would teach his principles to dozens of therapists. Although he started out believing psychoanalysis was the best way of helping others with their neuroses, he came to believe differently. He discovered that when he saw clients only once a week or every other week, they progressed just as well as when he saw them daily.

Ellis decided the key to mental health was not dredging up painful memories, but combating negative behavior head-on. He took a more active role than Freudian psychoanalysts, interjecting advice and direct interpretations, observing that clients seemed to improve more quickly when he was direct with them. By 1955, Ellis had given up psychoanalysis entirely and instead concentrated on helping people change by confronting them with their irrational beliefs and persuading them to adopt rational ones.

> Neurosis is a high-class name for whining
> —Albert Ellis

Albert Ellis wrote seventy-five books, many of which were *New York Times* bestsellers. At the foundation of REBT are some key assumptions about the unique nature of human beings. They include:

- People condition *themselves* to feel disturbed, rather than being conditioned by external sources.

- People have a biological and cultural tendency to think illogically and to disturb themselves needlessly.

- Humans are unique in that they invest in disturbing beliefs and keep themselves disturbed about their disturbances.

- People have the capacity to change their cognitive, emotive, and behavioral processes; they *can* choose to react differently from their usual patterns, refuse to allow themselves to become upset, and train themselves so that they can eventually remain minimally disturbed for the rest of their life.

- Humans are self-talking, self-evaluating, and self-sustaining. When people turn their *preferences* into dire needs, emotional disturbances occur.

By 1982, Ellis' peers ranked him the second–most–influential psychotherapist of the last one hundred years, just behind Sigmund Freud. In 2007, the National Institute of Mental Health estimated that more than two-thirds of therapists follow the model he outlined: REBT, a learning model with the goal of establishing new and healthier habits and responses to adversity.

Coming Off "Cruise Control"

Where do our irrational beliefs come from? Some are cultural, some societal, some handed down from our parents as we observe them and are taught ways to respond. Every event, pleasure, or adversity we experience in life contributes to our ingrained belief system and, once we develop habits that become deeply held core beliefs, we rarely challenge them. Instead, we repeatedly *act* on them.

It's similar to when we first learned to drive a car. In the beginning we were so anxious and cautious we devoted our attention to each maneuver. But over time, driving became *automatic*, and we didn't have to consciously focus on it. Our illogical beliefs are so well-established and practiced they just *feel* right, though they may be completely wrong. It doesn't take long until we're turning our *preferences* into dogmatic, absolute "shoulds, musts, oughts, and demands," with disturbing results. These "musts or shoulds" turned inward can cause *depression*; turned outward, they can generate *anger*.

According to Ellis, emotional and behavioral difficulties occur when humans take simple preferences such as the desire for love, approval, or success, and turn them into *dire needs*. We tend to engage in self-defeating patterns that are fueled by irrational thinking. Blame is often at the core of emotional disturbance: blame of self, of others, and of the world.

The ABCs of REBT

At the core of REBT is the *A-B-C* theory of emotional functioning. The *A* stands for the *activating event* or adversity a person faces—some type of challenging life situation, such as a family problem, work issue, or any of the things we point to as the sources of our unhappiness. *B* stands for *beliefs*, and the evaluation of the activating event, especially the irrational, self-defeating beliefs that are the actual sources of our unhappiness. *C* stands for *consequences,* the neurotic symptoms and negative emotions (such as depression, panic, and rage) that come from our beliefs. Although the activating experiences may be quite real and may have caused real pain, it is our irrational beliefs that create long-term, disabling problems for us.

To help resolve or correct the natural progression of *A-B-C* leading to negative consequences, Ellis adds *D* and *E*. The therapist or the client him/herself actively *disputes* the irrational beliefs *(D)*, in order for the person to ultimately enjoy the positive psychological effect of rational beliefs and *expected* new behaviors *(E)*. Disputing one's irrational beliefs is the cornerstone of REBT. It pokes holes in those illogical convictions that have been ingrained in us. This is an exercise that helps us to stop being victimized by our own thinking.

RATIONAL EMOTIVE BEHAVIOR THERAPY

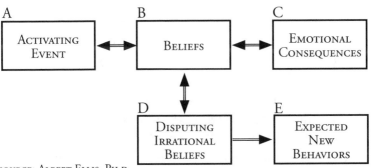

SOURCE: ALBERT ELLIS, PH.D.

Figure 13

Truthfully, it isn't necessary to pinpoint the source of these irrational beliefs, but we must acknowledge that they are the result of "philosophical conditioning," habits we develop as our predictable or automatic response to the tough issues in life. Ellis believes we are biologically programmed for survival to be susceptible to this kind of conditioning. Our beliefs take the form of absolute statements. Instead of acknowledging them as our *preference* or desire, we state our need as a fact and make unqualified demands on others to meet them—or convince ourselves that we have overwhelming needs that aren't being met.

> There are a number of typical 'thinking errors' people engage in: like ignoring the positive, exaggerating the negative, and overgeneralizing.

What are some of the absolutes *you* might think or believe? Perhaps that: "People must not take me for granted. Other people should behave in the way I want. I should be able to have what I want. The sun must shine tomorrow. I must not feel overwhelmed with responsibilities," and so forth.

There are a number of typical "thinking errors" people engage in, like *ignoring the positive, exaggerating the negative,* and *overgeneralizing.* If we're feeling depressed, we may refuse to see that we *have* had some successes in life and have some really good friends who love us. We may dwell on or blow out of proportion the *hurts* we have suffered. We may convince ourselves that nobody really loves us or that we always mess up. And often anger can be based on a faulty assumption that another person *should* behave as we want him or her to, instead of as he or she has chosen to act.

If you think about it, what the other person *should* do is not necessarily what he or she will do. A very important element of the equation is *reality.* They do what they do, and I automatically get angry about it and feel quite upset for awhile. It's like walking around with a big pushbutton on your forehead that says, "Push here to aggravate me." That's not a very useful response to others' behavior. Others are not *making* you feel or do anything; they are simply behaving in a way that angers you. The responsibility for the anger choice is yours.

Ellis gives twelve of the most prevalent irrational beliefs that cause and sustain unhealthy behaviors:

1. **The idea that it is a dire necessity for adults to be loved by all significant others,** instead of their concentrating on their own self-respect, on winning approval for practical purposes, and on *loving* rather than on *being loved*.

2. **The idea that certain acts are awful or wicked and that people who perform such acts should be severely damned,** instead of the idea that certain acts are self-defeating or antisocial and that people who perform such acts are behaving ignorantly or neurotically and would be better helped to change. People's poor behaviors do not always make them rotten individuals.

3. **The idea that it is horrible when things are not the way we like them to be,** instead of the idea that it is too bad, that we would better to try to change the bad conditions so that they become more satisfactory, and if that is not possible, we had better gracefully accept their existence.

4. **The idea that human misery is *externally* caused and is forced on us by outside people and events,** instead of the idea that neurosis is largely caused by the view that we take of unfortunate conditions.

5. **The idea that if something is or may be dangerous or fearsome, we should be terribly upset and endlessly obsess about it,** instead of the idea that one would better frankly face it and render it nondangerous and, when that is not possible, accept the inevitable.

6. **The idea that it is easier to avoid than to face life difficulties and responsibilities,** instead of the idea that the so-called *easy way* is usually much harder in the long run.

7. **The idea that we absolutely *need* someone stronger than ourselves on which to rely,** instead of the idea that it is better to take the risks of thinking and acting less dependently.

8. **The idea that to be worthwhile we should be thoroughly competent, intelligent, and achieving in all possible respects,** instead of the idea that we are imperfect creatures who have limitations and specific fallibilities.

9. **The idea that because something once strongly affected our life, it should affect it indefinitely,** instead of the idea that we can learn from our past experiences but not be overly attached to or prejudiced by them.

10. **The idea that we must have certain and perfect control over things,** instead of the idea that the world is full of probability and chance and that we can still enjoy life despite this.

11. **The idea that human happiness can be achieved by inertia and inaction,** instead of the idea that we tend to be happiest when we are vitally absorbed in creative pursuits, or when we are devoting ourselves to people or projects outside ourselves.

12. **The idea that we have virtually no control over our emotions, and we cannot help feeling disturbed about things,** instead of the idea that we have *real* control over our destructive emotions, if we choose to work at changing the poor hypotheses we often employ to create them.

Fortunately, everyone doesn't have all twelve of these irrational beliefs—or at least not all at the same time! But several can work in combination and result in a long-term, disabling, negativity within you. To get control of your mind, you must dispute them.

Some Disputing Techniques

Since these illogical beliefs are patterns from our past, they are so ingrained within us, for so many years that we can't just get rid of them by having a one-time, "Ah, ha!" moment. We need to work on disputing them every day for awhile, until they've been replaced by a new belief system. *How do you do this?*

Take out your journal, if you've been using one, and write down two or three of the illogical beliefs above that you think you may carry inside you, impacting your happiness. Or, to help guide you, write the words "often," "sometimes," or "never" after each of the twelve items to help assess which illogical beliefs currently affect you most.

Now, think of a current serious situation in your life that has been causing you a lot of emotional conflict—one where an illogical belief may be in use. Write it out, using the REBT formula *A-B-C-D-E:*

(A) What is the activating event?

(B) What are your thought processes, or underlying beliefs, about this activating event?

(C) What are the emotional consequences within you around this event?

(D) Now try disputing or challenging the irrational belief(s), substituting a rational belief for them instead.

(E) Then, ask yourself, if you were able to dispute the illogical idea, what new or different behaviors could be exhibited?

Let's use an example and a simple, six-step process to dispute a common irrational belief. In this example, think about someone who has not found their life partner, or someone who has been rejected by a close family member *(A)*. They feel angry, depressed, discouraged, dejected, defeated, and depleted *(B)*. Now, let's practice *disputing* the illogical belief that sustains these painful feelings:

1. **What self-defeating, irrational belief do I want to dispute and surrender?**

   A sample answer: "I must receive love from a person I really care for."

2. **Can I rationally support this belief?**

   Answer: No.

3. **What evidence exists of the falseness of this belief?**

   Answer: There are many:

   a) There's no law of the universe or social reality that says someone I care for must love me back . . . although I wish there were!

   b) If I don't get love from this person, I can still get it from others and find happiness.

   c) If no one I care for ever loves me (very unlikely), I can still find enjoyment in friendships, books, activities, work, whatever.

   d) If someone I care for rejects me, that will be unfortunate, but not life-threatening.

   e) At times in my life I have been unloved and yet am still happy.

4. **Does any evidence exist of the truth of this belief?**

   Answer: No, not really. Evidence exists that if I love someone dearly and never am loved in return, I will then find myself disadvantaged, inconvenienced, frustrated, and deprived. I would prefer not to get rejected. But no amount of inconvenience amounts to a horror. I can still stand frustration and loneliness. That hardly makes the world awful. No evidence exists that I must receive love from someone for whom I really care. In fact, many people don't, and they learn to accept it in some fashion.

5. **What are the worst things that could actually happen to me if I don't get what I think I must?**

    Answer: If I don't get the love I think I deserve:

    a) I would be deprived of certain pleasures.

    b) I would be inconvenienced by having to look for love elsewhere.

    c) I might never find the love I want and be forever deprived.

    d) Others might put me down and consider me worthless, and that would be annoying and unpleasant.

    e) I might have to settle for other pleasures than those I could have received in a good love relationship.

    f) I might remain alone much of the time, and that would be unpleasant.

6. **What good things could I make happen if I don't get what I think I must?**

    a) If the person I truly care for does not return my love, I could devote more time and energy to winning someone else's love and probably find someone better for me.

b) I could devote myself to other enjoyable pursuits that have little to do with a love relationship, such as work or hobbies.

c) I could find it challenging and enjoyable to teach myself to live happily without a love relationship.

d) I could work at achieving a philosophy of fully accepting myself, even when I don't get the love I crave.

One approach is to take one of your major irrational beliefs—your "shoulds, oughts, or musts" and spend at least five–to–ten minutes every day (for a period of several weeks) actively and vigorously disputing this belief. Maybe you can use an activity that you enjoy (television, computer, reading) as a reward by only allowing yourself to engage in it after you have practiced Disputing Irrational Beliefs for your five–to–ten–minute daily drill.

Another exercise is to tape yourself and try to listen more objectively to what you say. For example, "If I fail this job interview, that will prove I'll never get a good job, so I might as well apply only for low-level positions!" Figure out several disputes to this illogical belief, and strongly present them on this same tape. For example:

> "Even if I do poorly on this interview, it will only show that I failed this time, but will not show that I'll always fail and can never do well in other interviews. Maybe they will still hire me for the job. But if they don't, I can still learn from my mistakes. I can do better in other interviews, and I can finally get the kind of job I want."

Listen to your disputing on tape. Make sure you argue against these illogical beliefs, and do it passionately. When you see an attorney arguing for his/her client, don't they do it vigorously and with passion? Weak disputing won't work well to help you truly disbelieve some of your powerful and long-held beliefs, while persistent and vigorous disputing will. If you like, you can let other people listen to your tape, also, perhaps a supportive partner.

The following chart comprehensively covers the *ABCDE's* of REBT and may help in your daily disputing process.

ROADMAP TO HEALTHY BEHAVIOR

START WITH C, GO TO A, THEN WORK DOWN THROUGH B TO D, LEADING TO E.

A ACTIVATING EVENT	**B** BELIEFS	**C** CONSEQUENCES
DESCRIBE THE SITUATION THAT DISTURBS YOU "A" CAN BE INTERNAL OR EXTERNAL	IRRATIONAL BELIEFS LOOK FOR: • DOGMATIC DEMANDS (MUSTS, SHOULDS, OUGHTS) • AWFULIZING (IT'S HORRIBLE) • LOW FRUSTRATION TOLERANCE • SELF/OTHER DAMNING	UNHEALTHY EMOTIONS/BEHAVIORS • ANXIETY • DEPRESSION • ANGER • GUILT • SHAME • WORRY • COMPULSION
"A" CAN BE A PAST, PRESENT, OR FUTURE EVENT	**D** DISPUTE! IS IT TRUE? IS IT LOGICAL? IS IT HELPFUL? RATIONAL BELIEFS STRIVE FOR: • NON-DOGMATIC PREFERENCES, WISHES, DESIRES • EVALUATING BADNESS • HIGHER TOLERANCE • SELF/OTHER ACCEPTANCE	**E** HEALTHY EMOTIONS • CONCERN • SADNESS • ANNOYANCE • REMORSE • DISAPPOINTMENT • REGRET

Figure 14   SOURCE: ALBERT ELLIS INSTITUTE

REBT and Reality

Let's return to the people we met at the beginning of this chapter and use the REBT concept to examine their illogical beliefs. Remember Janice? Is it possible that her distress (and ulcers) over her stepdaughter's ingratitude was fueled by:

Illogical Belief #1: The idea that it is a dire necessity for an adult to be loved by all significant others.

Remember, the mind and body are intimately connected. When one suffers, the other sympathizes. Let's look at Figure #14. The *activating event* could be any number of things through the years. Let's just pick a simple one for now. Another Mother's Day rolls around, and she doesn't get a card. The activating event is: no Mother's Day card came from her stepdaughter. This causes her to think and remember all the *other* times she has been slighted and mistreated by this child, and so begin the negative emotions, and then the bad behavior, fighting with her husband about his daughter's lack of caring and respect. Her husband already feels terrible about his daughter's behavior, especially since Janice's children treat him so well.

She believes that the *(A)* activating event caused the emotions and behavior. The truth is, it was *(B), her beliefs* and thought processes that caused the emotions, which caused the bad behavior. What she needed to do was to *dispute her irrational belief that every significant person in her life needs to love her.* I understand that this is not an easy task for most of us. When we believe we have sacrificed so much for a loved one and that person doesn't appreciate our sacrifice, it hurts us to the core. But it doesn't have to determine our reaction to their unloving behavior. Now, go back and ask yourself some questions.

1. **Is there any evidence for this belief, and what is the evidence?** In this case, if you just look at the evidence

of "no Mother's Day card," that certainly might not be a big deal for many people, if they knew they were loved by this child. But, tie it to all the other ways this child has rejected her, and it's just one more hurt. If the evidence is *years of disrespect*, then there may well be evidence.

2. **What is the worst that could happen if you gave up this irrational belief?** It may be that Janice has to stop giving so much and stop showing her love, which isn't accepted anyway.

3. **What is the best that can happen?** Janice begins to understand both intellectually and emotionally that her self-respect is not tied to the love from this child and that her emotions are making her sick, which also affects her dealings with the rest of her family, who do love and respect her. Remember the *musts* and *shoulds* don't get us to change, anyway. It just puts considerable pressure on us from the inside to do something about something, which we are often unable to do.

Janice had to finally acknowledge that she could *want* her stepdaughter to love her, but it did not have to be a dire *need*. She couldn't demand it to happen. Janice used to review in her mind how different her life would have been if she hadn't taken this child into her home all those years ago. *If only she hadn't allowed herself to be so vulnerable in giving so much love and attention to this child.* But now, through this process, she began to realize that she didn't make the wrong decision to take the child into her home all those years. The person Janice is couldn't have done it any other way, and the love she gave was not in vain. It expressed her true nature. Since that love wasn't returned, Janice had to accept her stepdaughter's decision and let her go.

Now, let's look at Joe, Sr., and his anger at the bullies at his son's school. Could it have been triggered by:

Illogical Belief #2: The idea that certain acts are awful or wicked and that people who perform such acts should be severely damned.

The *activating event* was that his son came home from school upset about the bullies' fresh attack. Let's review the three disputing questions.

1. **Is there evidence for this belief, and what is the evidence?**
    Yes, there certainly is evidence that he is being picked on, but not necessarily that these kids are inherently wicked. We all know that there are wicked and evil people in this world that do horrendous things, but there are also people that are crying out for help and have such a low self-esteem that the only way they believe they can look good is by picking on others.

    My husband and I taught, as volunteers, a character-building program in two grammar schools, over a period of several years. One of the lessons was about being a bully. One of the questions we would ask was, "What would you do if you saw someone being bullied?" Typical answers were, "I would tell a teacher or another adult," or, "I would tell them to stop or try to make them stop."

    One little girl named Coral, in second grade, raised her hand and said, "I think I would want to talk to that bully to find out who hurt him so much that he had to try and hurt someone else." We were so impressed that we praised her for her answer and questioned how she came to that decision, saying how mature it was for someone her age to know this.

    Suddenly all these hands went up, and when called on the children would say, "You know, Mrs. Sweeny, what I would do? I think I would want to talk to them to find out why they did that. . . ." They all saw the praise she got from us and wanted it, too. Obviously, Coral was wise beyond her years—or perhaps she'd heard that answer from someone else, possibly her parents, and was repeating what she heard.

2. **What is the worst that can happen if Joe gives up this belief?** Maybe Joe, Sr., could learn something from Coral. If he gives up the hate and anger toward this child who ripped his son's shirt and stole his lunch money, he might begin to be grateful that his son is not the bully. As parents, we never want to see our children hurt—and the pain is sometimes worse for the parent, because we believe we are supposed to protect them. But Joe, Sr., can reduce *his* agony by understanding he is not in control of what someone *else* does and understanding he isn't in control of how his own child reacts to the situation. However in extreme cases, bullying can cause long term psychological problems for the victim and counseling may be warranted.

3. **What is the best that can happen?** Well, maybe Joe, Jr., takes karate and learns to protect himself from bullies. Joe, Sr, might then give up blaming himself, his wife, his son, and perhaps even the school system.

Remember Lauren, our corporate ladder-climber? Her distress about her boss' less–than–enthusiastic response to her ideas appears to be tied to:

Illogical Belief #3: The idea that it is horrible when things are not the way we like them to be.

1. **Is there evidence for this belief, and what is the evidence?** Yes there is evidence that she and her boss have some serious communication issues. However, her boss has not sat her down and given her a bad appraisal.

2. **What is the worst thing that can happen?** She could get fired. What if she does get fired? She will lose her salary and the benefits she needs for her children. She can't seem to think of anything else, and it's difficult for her even to have fun with her children. Lauren is having a pity party with herself, which is causing her to vacillate among constantly trying to please her boss, ignoring her, and being curt with her whenever she gets criticized.

3. **What is the best thing that can happen?** She could try some other things. Sit down with her manager and ask for a written review of her work objectives. Lauren may find that her manager thinks she is doing better than she thought. If not, they can discuss it in depth to see what she needs to do to improve. Perhaps her manager is envious or threatened by Lauren's new ideas.

   Maybe she could seek out someone in the human resources department with her concerns, or ask for a transfer to another department. Maybe her manager will get transferred or promoted—or leave the company. If Lauren does get fired, maybe she will find another job she likes even better.

Relentless Pursuit of Reality

As these case studies demonstrate, REBT provides a useful and practical way to think about and dispute untrue realities we may harbor in our minds. Ellis' concepts and techniques can be applied across a wide range of life situations. It's easy to understand why his model is so prevalent today! As we continue to get control of our minds, we will use this method for "disputing irrational beliefs" and to look at our emotions, challenging the habit of worry and fostering the art of forgiveness.

CHAPTER ELEVEN

PEOPLE: CREATURES OF EMOTION

"When dealing with people, remember: you are not dealing with creatures of logic, but creatures of emotion."
—Dale Carnegie

When Ellis wrote out his twelve illogical beliefs, I think he saved the best, worst, or *most problematic* one for last. Here's the belief we'll challenge now:

"The idea that we have virtually no control over our emotions and that we cannot help feeling disturbed about things—instead of the idea that *we have real control* over our destructive emotions, if we choose to work at changing the poor hypotheses we often employ to create them."

Of course there is no official "ranking" of Ellis' twelve irrational beliefs, but this one, which concerns our emotions, is outwardly demonstrative of the mental state that so frequently drives our emotions. It's responsible for a great deal of human suffering. I'd like to go deeper on the subject and discuss how we—both men *and* women—can better control our emotions.

That Little Voice Inside of Me

Did you ever admit to anyone that you hear voices in your head? A psychiatrist would likely call them "auditory hallucinations," and some might say they're a key sign of schizophrenia! Admit to a doctor, "I hear little voices in my head," and you may be committed to a psychiatric ward!

It's a little like those "crazy" people you sometimes come across in the street, incessantly muttering to themselves. (And I'm not talking about people on their ear-mounted cell phones!) Well, that's not much different from what you and I as "normal" people do, except that we usually don't do it out loud. The fact is that everyone hears voices in his or her head—all the time. They're *involuntary* thought processes, our own, continuous "self talk" or "internal dialogue." But what most of us don't realize is that *we have the power to control the dialogue.*

Our "inner voice" can be like a continuous monologue that comments, speculates, warns, scolds, judges, worries, complains, and expresses its likes and dislikes. The thoughts it speaks about may not even be relevant to a current situation; rather, they may involve a reliving of past events or the rehearsal or imagination of a possible future event. In some cases, the little internal voice imagines things going wrong and having negative outcomes. This is called *worry*, which we'll discuss later. And even if the voice *is* relevant to a current situation, it will interpret it in terms of past knowledge. That's because the voice belongs to your conditioned mind, which gets its information from your past history and the cultural mind-set you inherited from your family and environment; i.e., from *nurture* and from *nature*.

We see and judge the present through the eyes of the past, often getting a distorted view. Why? Because it is limited in its ability to see new possibilities based on information still to come. The voice, then, can be our worst enemy. It can drain us of vital energy and be the cause of unhappiness, misery, and even disease. Remember, the mind and body are intimately connected; when one suffers, the other sympathizes.

Where Do Emotions Come From?

Emotion, an activity of the mind as real as thought, arises at the place where mind and body meet. It is the body's physical reaction to a thought or, you might say, a reflection of your mind in the body. A hostile thought can create a buildup of energy in the body we call *anger*. Physically, our muscles may tighten, our focus may sharpen, and our heart rate may increase as the body gets ready to fight the thought that we are being threatened, either physically or psychologically. It's like the *fight or flight response* we experience during stress, discussed in Section I.

Fear may cause the body to contract automatically as it seeks to protect itself. Research shows that strong emotions, such as those provoked by trauma, can even cause permanent changes in the biochemistry of the body. Though, by listening to your own inner dialogue, you can "hear yourself think" at times, you are not always conscious of *all* your thoughts. Sometimes a physical symptom alerts you to a thought, such as breaking out in a sweat when you're not in a safe situation. Often through watching your emotions you can bring your thoughts into awareness. The good news is that you *can* free yourself from your thoughts and habitual mental patterns. You can intercept an automatic emotional response to a thought trigger and, thus, control your emotions more effectively. *How?*

Our mind is like a computer. We can program it to do whatever we want. And it's like a jukebox, too; the songs we choose to play over and over again we learn by heart, feel familiar with, and become attached to, like "old friends." The question is, do we want to play a sad song over and over again—or try a new, happy song?

> Our mind is like a computer. We can program it to do whatever we want.

Breaking the Compulsion to Repeat What's Familiar

Eckhart Tolle, author of the *New York Times* bestseller, *The Power of Now,* tells us we don't have to be controlled by our mind's old messages. The technique he suggests is that when we hear the voice (our mind's thought) in our head, we separate ourselves from it and make ourselves a third-party witness to the event of our mind having a thought. Then, as you listen to your thought as an outsider, you will be able to feel a conscious presence—your deeper self—behind or underneath the thought, so to speak. When you see your deeper self as separate and in control, the single thought loses its power over you and can subside, because you are no longer energizing the mind through identifying with it. You might realize something like this: *I am a person having a thought, but I am not my thought. I am much more than this thought, and I choose not to let it control my emotions.* This is the beginning of the end of involuntary and compulsive thinking.

Tolle says that when a thought subsides, you experience a discontinuity in the mental stream—a *gap of "no-mind."* The inner dialogue is paused as the deeper self evaluates it. At first the gaps will be short, perhaps only a few seconds, but gradually they will become longer. When you stand back and witness your thoughts, you can create that gap in the mind stream by directing the focus of your attention on "now." You stop the forward motion of past "old tapes" and force yourself to become intensely conscious of the present moment. *How does this work in everyday life?*

Well, for example, I love the beach and the ocean. Sometimes I am sitting on the beach enjoying the sun or riding the waves, and I lose that wonderful, present moment by allowing my mind to float into negative thoughts about something else that's happening in my life. When I realize it, I immediately stand back from the *negative thought flow* and observe those thoughts, then intentionally let them go so I can get back to the present moment of enjoyment. By choice, I no longer allow my mind's negativity to ruin the beautiful moment I'm having. Identification with the mind *("I am my thought")* and its encumbering baggage gives it more energy; but observation of the mind from a detached perspective *("I'm a person having a thought, and I can choose to set it aside")* drains energy from it and can help give control of your emotions back to you.

Like a computer throwing up every picture in my digital photo album on the PC screen as "wallpaper," my mind never stops going unless I'm completely engaged in some all-absorbing activity. I notice this most keenly when I have my bi-weekly massage to relieve the nagging symptoms of fibromyalgia. As I lie on the table, in a pleasant room with soft music, I know I'm supposed to be relaxed and let my mind go free so I can just focus on the healing touch of the massage. But that seldom happens. Instead, my mind runs from one thing to the next, either what I need to do next or what I didn't do that I should have done, etc. Sometimes it's a problem I can't find a solution for, and thus I can't stop thinking about. Maybe it's something I said to someone that I think may have hurt their feelings—or something that was said to me that did hurt mine. Meanwhile, as I focus on all these "problems" compulsively, I'm missing the enjoyment of the moment!

A technique for getting in the present that works for me is to picture a big red octagonal *stop sign*. It helps me to actually stop whatever thought processes I'm having and begin to be *in the now* and enjoy the massage or other pleasant moments. Sometimes I have to "raise my stop sign" two or even *three* times an hour. Reflecting on Tolle's approach to increase the "gaps of no mind," the more I practice being in the present *intentionally,* the longer I can halt the default, "wallpaper" mode of the unfocused mind and can remain in the present.

Getting Over Myself—Mentally

Why do we give so much control to our subconscious mental patterns, with all the past experiences and emotions that are linked to them? Perhaps it's because our individuality or *concept of self* is a belief system within each of our minds that we've molded over a lifetime and identified as being our ego. It survives by maintaining rigid boundaries, borders, filters, and limits on everything it sees, making current events comply with its established pattern, with life and human motives as we understand them.

For example, if someone at the office doesn't acknowledge or say *hello* as they pass you, or if two people are whispering at their desks and, when you approach, they immediately stop talking, your mind might automatically tell you, *Well, you did something wrong again,* or, *Those two must have been talking about you, which means they don't like you, which is the story of your life.*

Maybe you get a call from the school that your son is in trouble for the third time this year. Your mind starts talking to you: *What a lousy parent you've been. You can't even control your own child. You think you have tried everything, and nothing seems to work. How come others can do it for their children? What is going to become of him? If he doesn't get better grades, he won't get into college, and then he'll never get a good job. And without a good job, he will never be able to take care of himself. You'll be taking care of him forever. How embarrassing it is having to go back again to see the school principal and counselor.*

And then your automatic, negative emotions kick in: embarrassment, fear, anger at yourself, fury at your child, etc., etc. By defining its particular patterns and borders, the ego gives the illusion that *it* can tell you what is right and wrong, all in an effort to control you and instruct you on what you are and *are not,* how you should act and not act, and why you should judge those who challenge it. Because you learn from the outside world, you believe the truth lies outside of you. Judgment and fear feed the ego, generating numerous weaknesses and limitations you believe you must defend as real. The more time you spend in defense of the ego and its limitations, the more you believe that this is who you really are. And because you see the "you that you've created" as real and representing yourself, you defend it against anyone you perceive as attacking it.

Like most of us, you may feel that by defending your beliefs, even your irrational ones, you get stronger. And yet the more you defend false beliefs, the more they weaken you! If you identify with a rigid position, and then it turns out you're wrong, your mind-based sense of self can be seriously threatened with annihilation. *This is what my parents taught me; this is what I've always believed; it must be true,* you may think, and yet your unexamined assumption may no longer be true in the ever-changing reality of *the now.*

Wars have been fought over strictly held, inflexible belief systems (and irrational ones), and countless relationships have been destroyed by them. However, once you stop identifying with your mind *("I am what I think"),* whether you are right or wrong, it makes no difference to your true sense of self at all. You can state clearly and firmly how you feel or what you think, but there will be no aggressiveness or defensiveness about it. In essence, your sense of self will be derived from a deeper and truer place within you, not just from your mind. The more time spent in defense of your ego-self, the more time you will exist in a state of confusion and feel unnecessary annoyance, anger, stress, sadness, and depression *("Why can't everyone just agree with me?").* Yet these emotions exist because you mistakenly believe, feed, and keep alive the idea that reality is correctly represented by your ego-self's projected thought-stream. It's a shallow, past-focused perspective that leads to pain and requires course-correction.

To the ego, the present moment hardly exists, especially if the present contradicts the ego's belief system. Only the past and future are considered important. Ego is always concerned with keeping the past alive, because without it, who would you be? It is also concerned with the future, because that is when things will get better—when you get married, when you get that dream car, when you have children, when they grow up or have more time, when you get that promotion and have more money, when you retire . . . then you'll be happy! *Right?* Well, maybe. There's something to be said for deferred gratification, for getting an education to prepare for a career or saving money to buy a home. Projections of future happiness are fine, but not when they cause us to lose perspective and be dogmatic about *what we know* or lose openness to the present moment of time and relationship in the now.

> Wars have been fought over strictly held, inflexible belief systems, and countless relationships have been destroyed by them.

So, how we feel shouldn't be determined by our past experience, by our imagined future, by how people treat us, by our wealth, by our family situation, or by our job. With practice, we all have the power to manage our own emotional state, to live in the present, to foster positive instead of negative and destructive emotions, and to challenge and diminish the power of our irrational belief system, which triggers those negative emotions. Now let's apply the concept of "emotional control" and living in the present to one of the most difficult and prevalent problems we all face: how to have healthy and successful relationships with others.

Ain't Love Grand?

When I was in college I became fascinated with the subject of romantic love and "the *new hot*," as I called it, that first feeling you get when you meet someone you are extremely attracted to. Of course, who didn't? Every popular song (this was long before rap and hip hop) had to do with falling in love. I decided to do a research project on the subject for a psychology course I was taking. Here's what I learned. . . .

The initial euphoria of "love" is so wonderful, so energizing! You want to be with the person you've identified as "the one" all the time, tell them everything about yourself—and you want to know everything about them. You want to share *everything,* and as a duo you are always on your best behavior. You tend to see all the good qualities and none of the bad in your new partner. You just know that if you could be with that person forever that everything in your life would be wonderful. . . .

My research findings, based on case studies of fifty men and women, concluded that the "euphoric feeling" lasts somewhere between three months and three years. I found that the shorter, three-month mark of rapid "euphoria-loss" usually occurred when a couple lived near each other and were free to be together often. The slower, three-year mark occurred when either they lived far apart geographically or when one or both were not available to meet freely. Whether it was three months or three years, however, there always came a point where one began to see all the negative things he or she didn't see in the beginning, possibly because both began to let their defenses down and stopped always trying to be on their best behavior. Sometimes the other party didn't live up to the *idealized* model their partner had created for them and expected them to be.

At this point, my lovers either decided they were moving on to the next "new hot" (like the serial monogamist who gets a new marriage partner every three years!) or that the faults they had now discovered were minor things they could adjust to and live with. Some realized they had faults, too, or believed that this was his or her soul mate—the one they wanted to spend the rest of their life with—so, a few faults would have to be realistically accepted, along with the more essential qualities of the chosen partner.

I found that this same process of euphoric "first love" or "new hot" was the same no matter the pairing—where there were differences in age, color, religion, culture, or gender. And yes, even people over seventy had the euphoric feeling a "new hot" can generate.

Sometimes that special relationship seems to be the answer to all of the ego's problems and seems to meet all its needs. All the other things you derived happiness from before now seem insignificant. This person is now the single focal point that gives meaning to your life and defines your identity. And yet this "over-focus on the other" has a dark side, as well.

If in your relationship you experience love and the opposite of love, *emotional violence*, it is likely that you are confusing *addictive clinging* with love. In this case, often called *codependence*, your partner behaves in ways that fail to meet your needs. The feelings of fear and pain that had been covered up by the "love," or, "*new hot*" now resurface. Just as with every other addiction, you are on a high when the drug (your love, as you project him/her) is available, but invariably there comes a time when the drug no longer works for you.

When the painful feelings reappear, you feel them even more strongly than before—and you now perceive your partner as the cause of those feelings. By projecting your feelings outward and attacking the other, whom you believe is the intentional perpetrator of your pain, you hope this attempt at manipulation will be sufficient punishment to induce your partner to change his or her behavior. But your attack may just awaken your partner's own pain and provoke the launch of a counterattack of his or her own.

Addiction arises from the unconscious refusal to face and move through one's own pain. Every addiction starts and ends with pain. Whatever the substance—alcohol, food, drugs, a person—you are using something or somebody else to cover up your painful emotions, rather than face and deal with them. That is why after the initial euphoria has passed there may be unhappiness and pain in intimate relationships. Intimate relationships don't cause pain and unhappiness; they bring out the pain and unhappiness that is already there.

When your pain is deep, you have a strong urge to escape from it rather than surrender to it. You don't want to feel what you feel. What could be more normal than to move away from hurtful feelings? But there is no escape from painful, wounded emotions; only processing of the hurts that caused them can ease them permanently. Work, anger, drugs, suppression, projection don't free you from the pain. When you deny emotional pain, everything you do or think, as well as your relationship, becomes contaminated with it. You're stuck in the mire of "old tapes," telling you you're a prisoner of someone else's cruelty. *But how can you get free?*

When there seems to be no way out, there is still always a way *through*. The way through is to face the pain, to feel it fully. Feel it, but don't *think about it!* Express it, but don't create a repetitive script in your mind around it. Pay attention to the feeling you are having *in the now,* not to the person, event, or situation that seems to have caused it. Don't let your mind use the pain to create a victim identity for yourself. Feeling sorry for

> When there seems to be no way out, there is still always a way through.

yourself and telling everyone your story over and over again will only keep you stuck in suffering.

I did some volunteer work in a women's shelter some years ago. Often a woman stuck in a relationship with an abusive partner feels there is no choice but to stay and be victimized. The mind, conditioned as it is by past abuse, always seeks to recreate what it knows and is familiar with. *Even if it is painful, at least it is familiar,* we think. It's like you know all the street names and road rules of Hell, *so why move someplace that could be even worse?*

Compelled to repeat a pattern learned in childhood, where she felt she was unworthy and deserved to be punished, a woman remains with someone who physically abuses her. Her situation is self-created, but who—or *what*—is the self that is doing the creating? It is a mental and emotional pattern from the past, a familiar *tape*, no more than that. Nobody chooses dysfunction, conflict, and pain. Nobody chooses insanity or abuse. They happen because there is not enough *presence* in a person to will to dissolve the pain and not enough light to dispel the darkness.

A Positive Perspective Promotes Inner Peace

Patterns or lessons repeat themselves because we choose *not* to learn from them. We may not know we have the choice to do so. Or, we make certain mistakes in life that we don't learn from . . . and so repeat them until we learn to make choices from a deeper part of our being—choices with greater love and forgiveness. Once you have learned what a particular pattern is about, it is no longer necessary to re-experience it. Why do they keep reoccurring in your life? Perhaps there is some kind of value they hold for you. They may tell a story you need told or justify later choices in your life, for example. When you see you are holding on to them, you see that *you can choose* to let them go, also.

Any action is often better than no action, especially if you have been stuck in an unhappy situation for a long time. If it was a mistake that you made, at least you learned something from it . . . in which case, it's no longer a mistake. It was a valuable lesson you learned through a painful process. If you remain stuck in it, you learn nothing. You can choose to let the emotions around it go and move on with the new knowledge.

Is fear preventing you from taking action? Acknowledge that fear, watch it, and place your attention on it. Be fully present with it. Doing so cuts the link between the fear (emotional response) and your thought about the danger. (That's why the women came to the shelter—because they were finally able to break the fear of leaving with the *greater* fear of remaining.)

Surrender Your Fear

Don't let the fear rise up and reign in your mind, presenting its threats of destruction. If there is truly nothing you can do to change your present situation and you can't remove yourself from it, then accept it totally by dropping all inner resistance. The false, unhappy self that loves feeling miserable, resentful, or sorry for itself can then no longer survive. This is called surrender. To *surrender* is to cease fighting against a perceived enemy.

Surrender is not weakness. In fact, there is great strength in it. Because only if you surrender your fear of a situation will you be free internally of the fear the situation generates. You may then find that the situation changes without any effort on your part. In any case, you will be free from fear. When I saw how Nelson Mandela reacted when he was wrongly imprisoned for decades, I believed he had done just that. He surrendered his body but not his soul, which is why he was always so positive and at peace, even behind bars. Similarly, the Apostle Paul, while imprisoned and tortured, wrote some of his most uplifting and joyful epistles, refusing to let his physical imprisonment confine his mind and spirit.

Whenever a disaster strikes or something goes seriously wrong—such as severe illness, disability, loss of a home or fortune, the breakup of a close relationship, the death or suffering of a loved one, or your own impending death, know that there is another side to it—just one step away from something incredible. That step is surrender. It doesn't mean you will become happy about your situation. You may *never* be happy about what happened, or is happening to you at this moment. But as you surrender warring against fear and pain, and accept what they are teaching you about life, these emotions will be transmuted into an inner peace and serenity that comes from a very deep place. It is the "peace of God, which passes all understanding" (Philippians 4:7). Compared to that, even happiness itself is a shallow thing.

If God, as each of us understands Him, is the Eternal Presence in everything and, "God is Love" (I John 4:8), then to love is to feel the Presence of God deep within yourself and within others. Hence *all* love is the love of God. Love is the supreme emotion.

Let me be sure to clarify one thing: You don't surrender to people who want to use you or manipulate you or control you. It is possible to say *no* firmly and clearly to a person—or to walk away from a situation and be in a state of complete inner nonresistance at the same time. When you say *no* to a person or situation, let it not come from *reaction* to them but from a place of insight and a clear realization of what is right or *not right* for you at that time

When someone does something to you that is designed to hurt, try not to go into unconscious reaction and negativity, such as defending yourself, withdrawing, or attacking. Instead, let their action *pass through* you, as though you were a solid but *permeable* wall. In this way you become invulnerable to the attacks of evil. You can still tell that person their behavior is unacceptable, if you choose to do so. But that person no longer has the power to control your inner state. You are then *in your power*—not in someone else's, nor are you controlled by your mind, submitting to your own thoughts and fears of the attacker.

"He who angers you, controls you," a wise proverb says. Once a man went to see the Eastern teacher Gautama Buddha, intent on getting him to react angrily by humiliating him with insults. "If someone offers you a gift and you decline to accept it," Buddha asked him, "who does it belong to?"

"The one who gave it," replied the man.

"Yes, so if I decline to accept your abuse, then does it not belong to *you?*"

Inner Peace

If you have worked on your mission and vision and melded it with your values and principles, it is likely you will succeed in your outer mission and, at the same time, succeed in your inner vision. When you have seen the limitation of both to create ultimate inner peace, however, you can give up the unrealistic expectation that even totally fulfilling your mission and vision should make you happy.

Is there a difference between happiness and inner peace? *Yes.* Happiness depends on conditions being perceived as positive; inner peace does not. There have been many people for whom limitation, failure, loss, illness, or pain, in whatever form, turned out to be their greatest teacher. Their loss taught them to let go of false self-images and superficial, ego-dictated goals and desires. It gave them depth, humility, and compassion. It made them more real, more authentically spiritual, and more human.

Jesus Christ said: "Do not lay up for yourselves treasures on earth, where moth and rust corrupt and where thieves break in and steal" (Matthew 6:19). As long as a condition is judged as *good* by your mind—whether it be a relationship, a possession, a social role, a place, or your physical body—the mind attaches itself to it and identifies with it. It makes you happy, makes you feel good about yourself, and it may become part of who you are. But nothing lasts in this world, "where moth and rust corrupt." As Jesus furthermore said, we can "gain the world, but lose our own soul" (Matthew 16:26).

Enjoying your blessings, but not holding on to them so tightly that you react with negative emotions when they move beyond your grasp, is a great step toward knowing inner peace.

The external condition that made you happy at one time can now make you unhappy. The prosperity of today becomes the overindulgence and empty consumerism of tomorrow. The happy wedding and honeymoon can become the unhappy divorce or the joyless coexistence. Happiness, like pleasure, may arise from our possession of outer things or acceptance of the little we have. But *joy* and *inner peace* radiate from within.

Pulling It Together

Whenever you are unhappy, there is the unconscious belief that the unhappiness will get you what you want. If your mind did not believe that *unhappiness works,* why would you create it? Though misery and crying may work for the infant in her crib, it's an illogical belief, at best, for an adult.

The fact is that negativity does *not work* later in life. Instead of attracting loving relationships and desirable conditions, it stops them from coming. Instead of dissolving undesirable conditions, it keeps them in place. What is negativity's purpose? To dissolve painful feelings. Who is keeping them alive? *You are!* When you are identified with negative thoughts and emotions, it supports the universal law that negative output attracts negative input, delivering pain through compulsive thinking.

You keep unhappiness alive by giving it time and attention, letting the tape play again and again in your mind. Not until you surrender the habit of replaying negative thoughts in your mind (which trigger negative feelings) do happiness, joy, and inner peace become a living possibility in your life. *How do you get there?*

Whenever you notice some form of negativity arising within you, such as anger, loneliness, or blame of another, look on it not as a failure but as a helpful *signal* that is telling you, *Stop!* Get out of your mind and be present in the now. Feel what is happening *now*, and let go of your negative pictures and the internal thought-stream—all that negative self-talk creates. Commit right now *not* to be controlled by your own *personal thinking rituals* or caught up in habitual ways of thinking that negatively impact your life.

"Illogical Belief-Busting" Exercise

Let's end with an exercise to help you get to your specific negative thought habits and target them directly for change. So, get pen and paper and begin:

Write down *five negative emotions* you have on a regular basis. It takes effort to feel those feelings: disappointment, anger, despair, discouragement, loneliness, jealousy, envy, fear, worry, unforgiveness, etc. Now, answer the following questions:

1. Are these emotions all coming from the same area of your life? (See: "7 Key Dimensions" discussion.)

2. If it involved relationships, are they all coming *from the same person* in that key area of your life?

3. Can you *surrender* to that feeling or person so that the person or circumstance can no longer affect you in that negative way?

4. Can you identify any positive outcomes that have resulted from your suffering, perhaps as you find these in *God's goodness revealed through suffering* in *The Holy Bible* or in other inspirational reading, discussion, or prayer?

Finally, write *five positive emotions* you have on a regular basis, i.e.: love, generosity, empathy, gratitude, joy, excitement, humility or thinking about all you have and picturing God's goodness in all things. Are all of these emotions coming from the same area of your life? Do they come from an outside thing or person in your life? Do you find they arise from a deeper place within? Do you see how you can choose to access that deeper place by focusing on it now?

Moving Past Your Past to Personal Power

Emotional control is a very intense topic. In some ways we don't mind when we are controlled by our emotions, especially when they are positive ones—like happiness, love, excitement, enthusiasm. But negative emotions and pain also come to each of us in life. We live in a world that contains pain, yet it need not control us. *But how can we escape it?*

Pain lives in the past that is in you, alive because you keep it alive in your mind. If you identify with it, you identify with the past. A *victim identity* is the belief that the past is more powerful than the present. Actually, the opposite is true!

Joy and inner peace are possible for those who process pain and negative emotions and leave them in the past, moving beyond these as a choice of the will. Insisting that another person or what *they* did to you is responsible for who you are now, for your emotional pain, or for your inability to be your true self, keeps you stuck in *Pain City.* The solution is personal power. When you realize that you—and nobody *but* you—are responsible for the choice to feel what you are feeling right now, and that you do have the power to choose a more positive emotion, you can experience true joy.

CHAPTER TWELVE

"THE WORRY TRAP"

"Worry doesn't empty tomorrow of its sorrow;
it empties today of its strength.
It saps today of its joy."

—Anonymous

"What, me worry?"

—Alfred E. Neuman

William Inge, the great American playwright, once said: "Worry is interest paid on trouble before it's due." Personally, I've paid a lot of interest in advance. As a mother, I always thought worrying just came with the territory. I now understand that *concern* is appropriate, and *worry* is not. But learning the difference didn't come easily for me, as you will see.

My son Michael decided to go into the Peace Corps after college. He was sent to Guatemala at a time of some political unrest and was living in a remote village, five hours from the nearest telephone. Of course, he had no car, and there were no cell phones or Internet service, so there was no easy way for him to get in touch with me—unless he hitchhiked to the town of Salama and, even then, he could only call out "collect." Hence, there was no way I knew how or *when* he was going to call.

Many times I would come home from work to find a message from a Spanish-speaking operator, saying there was a collect call from "Miguel." I would be so sad to have missed his call, but all I could do was write to him and hope I would be home the next time he called. I must admit that, at the outset, I was worried—big time. But over time, I found a way to replace worry with *concern*. I decided to fly the family down to Central

America once a year to meet with him, a positive action that all of us could look forward to. I also immersed myself in my job, which helped the daytime hours to fly by. I used the slower hours at night, when worry about Michael resurfaced, to turn to God and my faith. Sure, I was still concerned about him, but I didn't obsess over his situation and make myself and the rest of the family sick.

The Negative Effects of Worry

As with stress and other negative emotions, worry saps our energy, enervates us, and affects our health. Dr. Charles Mayo said, "Americans take more pills to forget more worries about more things than people in any other nation in history." That may very well be true. I've visited several third-world countries, and overall, people seem to be happier, despite their economic conditions. They seem to have fewer expectations and demands of life than Americans.

When we visited our son in his small town in Guatemala, we were able to socialize with some families in their homes. Most were simple thatched huts with two rooms and a dirt floor, with two adults and three or four children living in each one. I remember one of our hosts saying that Americans have more time and technology to see all that they can have and all they don't have, so they want and expect more. The mother of the family said, "Here we get up early and work all day till sunset, and then go to bed and get up the next day to do it again. We have all our children living in this little community, and everyone knows what everyone is doing all the time. We are happy."

According to the medical community, worry affects the circulation and the central nervous system. Doing lots of it, especially over long periods of time, certainly can make us sick, but mathematically speaking, it really doesn't make *sense* to worry. Psychologists and other researchers tell us that roughly forty percent of what we worry about will never happen, and thirty percent has *already* happened. (Some of you may say, "OK then; if I worry about it, odds are it won't happen!") Also, twelve percent of our worries are over unfounded health matters. Ten percent involve miscellaneous fretting over daily circumstances, which accomplishes nothing. *What's left?* Only eight percent! It appears that we're worrying ninety-two percent of the time for no good reason—and making ourselves sick doing so! By the way, worrying about the other eight percent really doesn't help those situations, either.

As a destructive emotion, worry typically doesn't stand alone. It often drags with it *other* negative emotions, such as anger. If you're worrying at the office, with the agitation this creates, you can easily come home and kick the dog, yell at your kids, or snap at your spouse. Conversely, if you're worrying about family matters, you may bring anger to the office, lashing out at employees who are unrelated to the root cause or event.

Worry often brings along its old pal, self-pity. So, in the midst of worrying over this perceived *awful life* that you have created in your mind, you ask, *Why me? It hasn't happened to my friends. Why does it always happen to me?* This is a pity party, and others are allowed to come only if they bring gifts—like sympathy or words like, "I don't know how you manage." Some have mastered the art of dumping their problems on others in the guise of "sharing." The real masters don't do it directly; they're more subtle about it. But sometime shortly after they unload and depart, the recipients of their negative stream of worried and depressed content realize that they are now completely depressed, too.

Is Worry Logical?

In retrospect, it's easy to say we shouldn't have worried about this or that. We may regret wasting time needlessly worrying and making ourselves ill. *Then why do we keep doing it?* Do you recall:

> **Ellis' Illogical Belief #5:** "**The idea that if something may be dangerous or fearsome we should be terribly upset and endlessly obsess about it**—instead of the idea that one would do better to face it and render it non-dangerous, and if that is not possible, accept the inevitable."

So, worry is just another illogical belief to dispute. It's one of the major forms of negative self-talk mentioned in the last chapter. Let me ask you to do something right now. Take thirty seconds and *don't* think about a matter you recently worried about. . . .

How did you do? You probably could think of little else except whatever it was you recently worried about. Telling someone "not to worry" is useless and unproductive, like telling someone to "just stop smoking" or drinking or practicing any other destructive habit. While Jesus said, ". . . don't worry about tomorrow, for tomorrow will worry about its own things," (Matthew 6:34, paraphrase), many of us still worry about the past, present, *and* the future, giving credence to the old saying, "Today is the tomorrow you worried about yesterday."

> Today is the tomorrow you worried about yesterday.

Worry *vs.* Concern

Most think worry is just a normal human activity; after all, everyone worries, *don't they?* But worry, one of the major forms of negative self-talk, is actually a destructive mental habit. In fact, worry may shorten one's life, as the origin of the word suggests.

In Old English, the root of the word *worry* was *wyrgan,* which meant "to strangle." Its Middle English descendant, *worien,* retained that same concept and developed it even further; it meant, "to grasp by the throat with the teeth and lacerate," or, "to kill or injure by biting and shaking." Not a very pleasant picture, is it? Today's dictionary still lists those two definitions, but the main one now reads: "to feel uneasy or concerned about something, to feel anxious, distressed, or troubled."

Many today use the words *concern* and *worry* interchangeably because they're similar mental activities. Both take a lot of energy and tend to focus on an important issue, but behaviorists see a distinct difference between *concern* and *worry.* Naturally, we should be *concerned* when a friend or family member is sick or is going through other trials or personal challenges. Concern is a purposeful thought pattern that promotes constructive and healthy behavior. If we're *concerned,* we assess the problem and go to work on fixing it. Concern is characterized more by forward movement and seeks to advance us in growth and maturity. That's a productive way to channel our energies. By contrast, worry is an obsessive habit, characterized by internal mental gymnastics that run

> Worry is like a rocking chair. It requires a lot of energy, and it gets you nowhere.
> —Leo Buscaglia

our thoughts in repetitive circles, with very little forward progress. As Leo Buscaglia, the inspirational author, said, "Worry is like a rocking chair. It requires a lot of energy, and it gets you nowhere."

When we replay the same negative story line, we often extend it to further negative consequences. Let me give you a classic example. I have a friend who constantly worries that her only son will be involved in a tragedy or terrorist attack that will take his life—just because he works in New York City. And then, extending that worry, she imagines that his young wife will probably move back to the Midwest, near *her* mother, with the children, and then she will remarry . . . and then my friend will rarely see her grandchildren. She's created a string of hypothetical, negative scenarios and consequences, extending them far into the future—all based on an illogical fear!

Some people become chronic worriers and are so used to worrying that when they have nothing to worry about, they worry about that! Society calls these people "worry warts." Sometimes our culture is actually supportive of worry because of its inappropriate connection with *caring*. If you tell someone you're not worried about an issue, they may wonder if it's because you don't care about it. *Are you just apathetic,* they may wonder? But worry is not a sign of caring; *concern* is the real companion of caring, because it is proactive.

Who's in Control?

Another key factor that keeps us addicted to the habit of worrying is the illusion that as long as we are worrying we are affecting the outcome of a distant circumstance, thus we can exercise some *control* over it. As humans, we want to have a sense that we are controlling our own destiny. We may become miserable when our life, or an important person in our life, feels *out of our control.* So, worry fills in as a mental activity that gives us a false sense of control as we focus on the things in life that we actually have no control over.

Why do we spend so much time trying to control the very things that are out of our control? It's inherently fruitless, but we can't accept the truth that *we don't control the universe;* thus, we must learn to accept some things that are beyond our power to influence.

In contrast to worry, exercising *concern* towards things expends energy dealing with things that *are* within our control. For the rest, we can proactively choose to, "Let go and let God." As the opening of Reinhold Niebuhr's "Prayer of Serenity" asks:

"God, grant me the serenity to accept the things I cannot change,
the courage to change the things I can,
and the wisdom to know the difference."

The "Happiness Gene"

Why do some of us worry *more* than others? Often we're not aware how the *worry habit,* with its destructive chain of spiraling fearful thoughts, even began. Did we pick up this habit watching our mother or father react in kind? Was it enjoined by our teachers: "You *should* be worried about getting into college," or is it just *inborn?* Actually, it's all of these things.

One baseline study on human happiness was reported in an article by Kathleen McAuliffe, in *The Self Journal,* December, 1996, entitled "Born to Be Happy?" McAuliffe reported that researchers found no matter what happens to us, good or bad, we return to the level of happiness predisposed by our genes. This is what scientists call our "set point," or our personal baseline for happiness.

This conclusion stems from research based on interviews and analysis of the lives of 2,300 twins. Psychologists at the University of Minnesota asked subjects to evaluate their present level of happiness, then compared their ratings with those of the general population. It turned out that genetically identical twins—even those *separated at birth*—were much more likely than fraternal twins or other close siblings to come up with similar ratings of happiness. Researchers estimated that roughly *half* of our sense of wellbeing is due to inherent genetics. Family income, level of education, marital status, and religious affiliation had a negligible impact; in fact, less than three percent!

Even when catastrophe strikes, it seems that people soon return to their emotional "set point." Two University of Illinois psychologists, Edward Diener and Carol Diener, observed that within three weeks of suffering a spinal cord injury, more than half of those afflicted report that happiness is their strongest emotion. Some experts caution us against relying too heavily on the results of a few studies, but others expect the findings to hold up: "Happiness strongly correlates with optimism, extroversion, and the absence of neuroticism—personality traits all known to be genetically influenced," says behavioral geneticist Robert Plomin, M.D., of the Institute of Psychiatry at the University of London. If genes do account for about *half* of our happiness, then experiences unique to the individual account for the rest, which leaves a lot of room for self-improvement. We can undo negative patterns of thinking, although it may just take more work for some of us. Genes provide us with the *hardware* for happiness, but the *software* comes from social learning.

This research correlates with my own experience in life. I've known many people who always seem to be happy, content, and positive—even in dire circumstances. And yet some others who appear to have everything—good health, loving family, no financial problems—are *never* happy or content. Spend a day around an optimist and a pessimist, and you will note the difference in how each sees and reacts to the world. It's not what the world does to them, but their *perception* that makes for unhappiness.

Two of Ellis's Illogical Beliefs relate to this subject:

Illogical Belief #3: "The idea that it is horrible when things are not the way we like them to be—instead of the idea that it is too bad, that we would be better to try to change the bad conditions to be more satisfactory, and if that's not possible, to gracefully accept their existence."

And . . .

> **Illogical Belief #4:** "The idea that human misery is invariably externally caused, forced on us by outside people and events—instead of the idea that neurosis is largely caused by the view that we take of unfortunate conditions."

"Worry" Develops Environmentally—*At Home, School, or Work*

So, the habit of worrying is partly *nature* or hereditary, and it is partly *nurture,* or environmental. I grew up with a mom who "fretted" about little things but didn't really worry, and a dad who never worried about anything. Mom was a loving and empathetic person who gave to everyone around her. She gave of her time, her treasure, and her talents. Her empathy was so strong that it made her concerned for others, which led to actions designed to support them.

My dad was a strong, hardworking, pragmatic businessman, and unabashedly self-centered. He did what he wanted, when he wanted, and how he wanted. However, in a crisis, my father and mother were both equally strong. Our most memorable crisis entailed the destruction of the family business due to a major burglary.

My parents owned a jewelry store in Newark for over thirty years. During the last ten years the store was open, the city was experiencing a serious economic downturn. Racial riots ensued, and as the inner city deteriorated, many residents and businesses moved out. My parents relocated their home to the suburbs but decided to keep the store open in Newark for just a few more years in order to serve the clientele they knew so well. It was the mid 1960s, and my father was seventy-five-years-old—too old to start again someplace else.

In July of 1965, we got a call from the police one morning at 5:30 A.M. The store had been robbed! When Dad arrived, he found that the robbers had been in the store since he'd closed on Saturday evening at 6 P.M. They'd bypassed the upstairs alarm, climbed down the wall, and spent the next thirty-six hours blowtorching the vault open. When they finally left, at 5 A.M. Monday morning, they triggered an emergency alarm they didn't know about.

We lost almost everything that fateful day, every piece of jewelry that was in the vault, including people's jewelry on consignment, my mom's personal jewelry, furs, bank money orders, and cash. Ironically, my father had millions of dollars in fire and burglary insurance coverage on the front of the store, but none on the vault, because it was supposedly "burglar proof!" My father lost his entire life savings, a million dollars, that day—or probably five–to–ten million dollars in today's economy. I remember my father calling us when he got down to the store and crying into the telephone.

"Margaret, we're wiped out. We've lost everything," he said. Mom and I immediately drove down to the store and pushed our way through the throng of police, TV cameramen, and newsmen, just as they were interviewing my father. After a few hours my Mom, who was completely calm, said, "Susanne, let's go around the corner and get a cup of coffee." As we were sitting there drinking our coffee, a school group of blind children came into the diner and my mom looked at me and said, "You see, honey, that's a problem. What we have isn't a problem. It's just *money*. Your father could have been killed, but fortunately he wasn't there. We'll be OK."

I guess we all have certain moments when a parent has said something to us that is especially meaningful and memorable. Well, that was certainly one for me! My parents altered their lifestyle tremendously after that. They sold their home and moved into their little summer bungalow, where they lived for the rest of their lives. They never complained, not once! My dad was depressed about it for maybe a few weeks, but he got over it. My mother never blamed him for not moving out of Newark sooner, as she had asked him so many times to do, and never reproached him for failing to have the right type of insurance in place. They served as good role models in teaching me, by example, not to worry, especially about material things, and also not to harbor bitterness.

So, neither by nature *nor* by nurture did I have an innate propensity to worry, but later, after my seven-year-old son had the terrible accident, I began to get into the *worry habit*. I think that was when I realized that bad things don't just happen to *other* people; they can happen to me, also. It makes one realize how vulnerable all humans truly are. On the other hand, it also makes you realize you can get through anything and be stronger for it. Adversity, when not permitted to destroy you, really does make you stronger.

Some people may worry about their health, finances, or career. For me, worry was always about my children. I didn't worry about finances or my career, because I believed there was always something I could *do* about those things. I didn't worry too much about my health, though over the years I'd been told I might have ovarian *and* lung cancer. I had the hysterectomy but, thankfully, no cancer. Cat scans of my lungs showed some problem areas that shouldn't be there in someone who didn't smoke, didn't live in a third world country, and had never had tuberculosis. Twice a year for *years* I had to continue with scans to make sure those "problem areas" didn't get worse. I am not saying I wasn't frightened at times, but I didn't *worry* about my health, despite these circumstances. I took action on it.

Since I am an only child, I was the caregiver for my parents the last ten years of their lives. Dealing with Mom's Alzheimer's and Dad's physical deterioration after he broke his hip and could no longer walk was very difficult, especially while taking care of my own busy family and career. I felt tired, sad, frustrated, even *overwhelmed* with all that had to be done, but

I don't remember *worrying* about it, even when I found out, through blood work, that I had the Alzheimer's gene. It was a *concern,* but not a worry. I continue to take action on this concern by participating in an Alzheimer's research study group, and I leave it at that.

But with my children, it's a different story. For years, whenever I heard an ambulance siren, I instantly worried that the emergency involved one of my children. Those of us who have teens know that when we get a call in the middle of the night it's going to be bad news. Of course, we expect that as our children grow up, the parental tendency to worry about them must surely subside. Well, it doesn't!

My son Jeff lives in the woods of Connecticut, in a house by himself, out of sight from the nearest neighbor. As a young adult he decided to save some money one summer by re-roofing his two-story house himself. The roof is steep and slippery, and of course, he would be using power tools. Needless to say, it didn't take my imagination long to create a full-length disaster movie. *What if he falls off the roof or seriously hurts himself? I thought. No one will be there to help him, because he is alone.*

Fortunately, Jeff always carries his cell phone for work. So, when he was repairing his roof I called his cell phone. No answer. I called again and again. Nothing. *That's it; he's fallen! Who should I call?* Time for my mental "stop sign" again! And time for me to catch my breath and substitute more logical concern for worry. Of course he didn't fall or have a heart attack. His cell phone battery had gone dead!

The negative information overload we get twenty-four hours a day, seven days a week, through TV, radio, Internet, and newspapers can be fraught with major catalysts for worry. When we worry, we choose to use our imagination in a way other than the way it was created to be used. We create negative "what if" scenarios. *What if I lose my job? What if I can't get another one? What if I get sick and there is no money? What if my child never finds anyone to love him or her? What if my child can't get a decent career?*

And on and on and on. . . .

"Post-9/11 World" Responses and Phobic Fears

Of course, worry isn't confined to family issues. Some worry about world events or obsess on the possibility of global catastrophe of epic proportions. Think about people's widely varying responses to terrorism and threats of terrorism.

After 9/11, many individuals and companies moved out of New York City, fearing something similar would happen again since NY was clearly the #1 target of terrorist activities and remains the media, financial, and cultural capital of the world. And yet, many stayed put. In fact, the city is now growing again, and real estate values are soaring, especially downtown, close to "Ground Zero."

I've always lived in the Tri-State area near Manhattan and have a strong allegiance to "the City." At one time or another, *all* of our children have lived there. One son, daughter-in-law, two granddaughters, and their dog *still* live there, and like most New Yorkers, they love it, won't leave it, and don't stress or worry over what could happen again.

The couple married two months to the day after 9/11—and only a few blocks from the World Trade Center. The building they chose to be married in had overlooked the WTC, which was one of the reasons they chose the location. Almost everyone invited came to the wedding, but a few people were just too afraid to be in New York City, and some even feared ever flying again.

Everyone has a different *worry factor*. Some people won't fly, some have a fear of bridges, others are just fearful of leaving their homes! Is it a problem? Well, if someone is very happy with her life without ever flying, then that fear or worry may not be affecting her life negatively. However, if she loves to travel and is paralyzed with worry about flying, then she *does* experience a loss because of entertaining an irrational fear.

So, how do we stop and reverse that negative thinking cycle that feeds on itself?

How to Reduce Worry—or Replace Worry with Concern

We've established that worrying is a habit, something that is involuntarily, and often unconsciously, repeated. And we know that habits become deeply ingrained when done for so long that you're no longer even aware of them. If worrying is a long-term or *chronic* problem for someone, it is likely because that person has done *a lot* of it in the past. So, as in breaking any long-held habit, it takes repeated practice of different courses of action, ones that are less compatible with worry.

Because each person is unique, the way in which he or she worries is unique. And so, the best way for each person to reduce worry may vary. What works for one may not work for another. Choose a method that works for *you,* and then practice it repeatedly. If the unwanted habit isn't changing after a few weeks, then try a different method of extinguishing it, and practice that for awhile—or try combining methods. Here are some techniques I think are worth trying:

1. **Observe yourself in the act of worrying.** Catching your worry early on is good, because the longer a "worry episode" lasts, the more the habit is strengthened. The more conscious you are of the habit of worrying, the greater the chance to *switch a thought off* before it becomes an obsession. Remember Tolle's concept of detaching yourself from your thought patterns in order to manage your emotional state? It's the same idea. The more we can sit back and watch our mind go off on us, the more we can understand what is happening and *choose to refuse* to give it any power. In learning to observe yourself worrying, it

may be useful to keep track of how often an episode of worry occurs during the day. Make marks on your calendar or journal to record the information. This will show you how much time you spend worrying each day. As you practice more awareness of worry-filled time periods and implement intentional worry-reduction skills, you'll get measurable feedback and see what affect your new methods are having.

2. **Limit your worrying to one part of the day.** Choose a time and place and limit worry to that time and place only. Perhaps you'll "let yourself worry" at the kitchen table at 8 A.M., but never just before bed. So if, in the middle of the day, you begin to worry about something, just tell yourself you are postponing that thought spiral to the kitchen table at 8 A.M. the next day, the official "worry period." Compartmentalizing the worry means that worry's negative content won't interfere with the important things going on in your day, and perhaps by the time you get to your "worry period," you may have forgotten an item or put it into better perspective. For those worries that you *can* do something about, the reserved time and place will be good for problem-solving.

3. **Track the outcome of your worries.** Write down every event you worry about, and list the possible outcomes that might soon happen, both good and bad. Keep the list, and after the event actually happens, see which outcome actually occurred. Over time you will be able to collect your own evidence about your worries, their validity, and your ability to cope. You will find out that few things turn out as badly as you thought they would, and that if they do, you probably are capable of handling them.

4. **Reframe circumstances as being "inconvenient."** I remember attending a conference twenty years ago. I can't even remember who the motivational speaker was, but his message was a single word. For nearly an hour, he said he was going to give the audience one word that could change our lives forever. He prefaced his revelation of the word with dozens of fascinating stories of people who overcame adversity or somehow put bad things into context and got on with their day, their week, or their lives. It turned out that the one word was simply "inconvenient." His message was that a huge percentage of the stress, anxiety, and worry-producing events that happen in life are *not* really life-threatening or life-altering. They're merely *inconvenient*. And that if you keep that message close at hand, the next time you miss a flight, get caught in traffic, suffer investment losses, even lose a job, just reframe the issue into a context of its merely being "inconvenient."

5. **Use cognitive restructuring.** Remember our discussion of Albert Ellis and REBT? He said: Identify the specific thoughts you worry about. What are you saying to yourself? Then, take each thought and analyze it logically. What is the evidence for it, and what is the probability of its happening? Is it reasonable and logical to predict that it will happen? What evidence do you have that it will? If the event happens, will you be able to handle it? Have you had situations in the past like this without terrible consequences? A year after the event, what difference did it make in your life? Find evidence that indicates the likelihood of things working out and shows you will have ways of coping with the event if it happens.

6. **Exercising faith and practicing meditative prayer** are major ways to stop worrying. This last technique really

works well for me and reinforces my own personal vision statement, so I'll go into this one more deeply.

The Power of Faith

Over the past decade, researchers who study psychological resilience have developed new respect for the role of religious faith and prayer in helping people cope with trauma and life trials. Like you, I've seen dozens of examples in my life.

A *USA Today* headline on July 19, 2007, said it all: "The Lord is Her Bulwark against Rising Troubles," it proclaimed. The article explained how a Katrina survivor was standing fast in her faith. She had lost her home in the flood disaster, only one year after the death of her husband. Last fall, her son had committed suicide. Then, robbers broke into her trailer and took what little she had left. During all this, her faith in God has only grown stronger. "This is what sustains me," she stated. "When it's really bad, you put it in His hands. You do what you are able to do and have faith that He can do the rest. He's carried me on many days when I couldn't walk myself." You don't have time to worry when you're practicing your faith actively.

A wonderful friend, John, died of bone cancer at the age of thirty-three, leaving his wife and six-year-old son. His loving wife, Grace, said to him one day in despair, "Why *you*, John? I just don't understand." His answer was, "Why not me?" His faith gave him the strength to push through some serious pain so he could spend more time with his son, Doug, leaving him more memories of his dad. John also used his last three years of illness to share his faith with others and to read and *reread* every page of the Bible, which at his death was filled with notes and insights on every page. That was one of the things he left to his son, along with the legacy of being a faith-filled father and a man of tremendous caring and courage. And he had absolutely no self-pity. When my husband and I would visit him at home or in the hospital, John always wanted to know how *we* were doing.

My good friend, Gloria, lost her twenty-three-year-old daughter in an auto accident caused by a drunk driver. Through her horrendous shock and grief, she only drew closer to God, and He gave her a ministry to help others that had experienced the loss of a child. That ministry, "Growing through Grief," had a support group that met every month. Instead of each attendee going over their tragedy and sorrow with the group, Gloria developed a program where each month a different topic would be presented and discussed . . . and always by an author, clergyperson, doctor, or social worker who had also lost a child. Examples of her topics were: "The First Holiday after the Death," "How to Deal with Grieving Siblings," "When One Parent Wants to Move on Sooner Than the Other." "Growing through Grief" was a positive, forward step for Gloria—and for every person whose life was touched through her faithful concern.

One of my lifelong friends, Judi, has had ten surgeries and twenty-four hospitalizations. Legionnaires disease, a kidney transplant, the EMV Virus, an E-Coli infection, gall bladder surgery, neuropathy, bursitis, serious leg and thumb injuries, hand surgery, two bunion operations, Peritonitis appendicitis and an umbilical hernia, a hysterectomy, diabetes, gout, tubal ligation, diverticulitis, and more. Here is what she says about the ordeals she's endured:

> "With the surgeries prior to my kidney trans-
> plant, I relied more on myself than on God to
> get me through. By the time of the transplant,
> I knew God was in total control of my recovery
> process. First, He provided a donor for me—
> my younger brother, Richard, who generously
> offered his kidney, without even being asked.

I never had to go on dialysis like most transplant patients. As part of God's perfect plan, my mother revealed to me that she had never understood why she'd had a third child, since she never had the desire for another child after I was born, but realized during the transplant surgery at least *one* reason she'd been given a third child had been to save my life. I realized each time I had surgery or was hospitalized that God was going to use my situation to draw more people to Himself. He used me many times in the hospital to show others faith, and the prayers of others got me through very serious illnesses.

My concerns over health problems have been placed entirely in God's Hands. When I had legionnaires disease, I was in the hospital with a fever of 104 degrees for five days. The doctors did not know where the source of the fever was coming from. After many tests and *no* answers, I realized this might just be the time of my death. I remembered from a Bible study that we can limit God's power to act on our behalf by our lack of faith, and by not putting all of our trust in Him. I asked Him that morning to "dazzle me." Then, I looked out of my hospital window and saw the most beautiful sunrise! The sky was pink–and–blue striped. I knew then that God was going to get me through this. My faith does waver at times when I can't even pray for myself, and that's when God has others pray for me. He never disappoints!"

In my studies on fear and worry, I found 366 incidents in Scripture where it says, "Fear not." *What?* I thought: *I can't help worrying and being fearful. But Scripture says I can. How do I do this: "Fear not"?* I learned that it has nothing to do with my feelings. Rather, letting go of fear is a choice—a choice to believe and trust in God, to believe His Presence is with me, and that in His Presence my fear and worry is swallowed up. "Let not your heart be troubled" (John 14:1).

The Power of Laughter

The use of humor can also be a tremendous resource in overcoming stress and worry. Laughter, in itself, has long been known to be a powerful, yet unexplainable, ingredient in treating serious diseases, including cancer. In fact, the popular television news magazine *60 Minutes* did a program on it almost two decades ago, showing cancer patients laughing at jokes about cancer in an intentional form of therapy. Results of this intervention were medically significant.

Dr. Lee Berk of California calls laughter one form of *eustress* (remember, the *positive* kind of stress discussed in Chapter One?). The University of Florida has done clinical trials in attempts to prove laughter's positive effects, finding them measurable. According to a recent article published in *Alternative Therapies in Health and Medicine,* laughter reduces stress and increases natural *killer cell* levels (a type of white blood cell that attacks cancer cells). Researchers are beginning to investigate other complementary and alternative medicine (CAM) therapies that may alleviate stress and improve immune response, such as meditation, yoga, massage, music therapy, and "laughter therapy."

Research findings demonstrate that *pain* is reduced by the very act of laughing. One explanation may be that laughter is simply a welcome distraction to pain that allows a person to forget about it for a moment and focus on something else.

But laughter also relieves pain by triggering the release of *endorphins,* chemicals in the brain that are natural painkillers. Laughter can fight fatigue . . . and we know it *definitely* relieves stress. Laughter has been described as "an internal massage of the organs" that stimulates digestion and circulation. Most people say they feel better during or immediately following a bout of laughter. So, stop worrying and keep laughing. It's really good for you!

Madeline's Gift

A vibrant personality with an infectious laugh, a quick wit, and often outrageous behavior . . . that's how I would describe Madeline. She's been a close friend for over twenty-five years now. Our sons also have been friends throughout high school, college, and now their adult years. As couples, we've skied together, traveled to Europe, rafted, partied, and frequently laughed till we've cried. Lately we are doing a little of both, and I'm learning from her resourceful use of humor.

A classic Maddy stunt occurred at the twenty-fifth wedding anniversary surprise party friends threw for her and her husband, John. Maddy figured out that "something was up," but never said a word. So when my husband and I arrived to pick the couple up to attend a "business function," she strolled down the staircase wearing her twenty–five–year–old wedding gown. It wouldn't close in the back and smelled like moth balls, but she wore it the entire evening—turning the tables on our "surprise party" by doing us one better!

Madeline has the greatest sense of humor in both good times and bad. Right now is one of those very bad times, however. Her cancer is back after seven years in remission. Ten years ago Maddy was diagnosed with ovarian cancer, had surgery, and underwent all the treatments that followed. She came out of it with the relief of a medical verdict of success and proclaimed herself fully cured. She didn't worry about it any longer and always spoke positively when asked about her condition. Even now, in this terribly tough time of re-onset, when she is so tired she can barely move, she still jokes about everything, including her situation. Maddy has a wonderful sense of humor not even cancer can take away from her, and that is her gift to us all.

A Personal Prayer Story

Two years ago I got a call from my son Michael (*yes,* the same one) telling me they found two melanomas on his body in a routine exam. I thought I was hearing him wrong. *Not melanoma. It couldn't be.* I've had basal cell and squamous cells myself. But not *melanoma;* it couldn't be! That's the deadly form of skin cancer, and he was only thirty-five-years old!

Nevertheless, one patch of melanoma was on the instep of Michael's foot. They had to go so deep to get it out that they needed to replace it with some other tissue and fat. Since he had no fat on him *anywhere* they had to remove muscle and tissue from his calf surgically. It would be weeks after the surgery before the results were known. He told me not to worry, explaining that the doctors thought they had caught it early enough. He and I, however, both knew that the little "freckle" he had on his instep had been there for at least eight years. He never had a bad burn, and I was in shock. Later we were to learn that the condition may have had something to do with a parasite he got in Guatemala while in the Peace Corps. It had taken a long time to get rid of the parasite, and Mike's immune system may have been compromised while he carried it.

Since I know that exercising *concern* is the way to go instead of worrying, I got every piece of information available on melanoma, some from friends who have had the condition themselves. I tried to talk to Michael about it, asking lots of logical questions ("How big? How deep? What stage is it? Shouldn't you go to a melanoma skin cancer specialist?"), but he wouldn't talk to me about it. He told me he was handling it and I needed to: "Stop worrying!"

My son had used the wrong word. Remember, with concern you are supposed to be able to *do* something; it involves linear movement and a journey towards growth and maturation. Concern is a thought style that promotes constructive and healthy behavior. But my son wasn't allowing me to be involved or to help him in his process of gathering information and making decisions. *What was left for me to do but worry?* You can imagine the fantasy I created in my mind. *What if they can't get it all? What if it has spread? What if he dies? What will happen to his young child? He is such a perfect father! How will this child and his wife survive? She will marry someone else, and the new husband won't let me see my grandchild. How will I survive? I don't want to survive if. . . .*

My "stop sign" signaled. What I did next was to turn to everyone I knew who would pray *with* me, and not just for me. I didn't need anyone to cry with me or sympathize with me or feel sorry for me. I needed my "problem" lifted up to the Lord. I needed my faith lifted up. I needed to "let go and let God."

So often I would give God my problem, and before the end of the day I would go and "take it back." I guess I thought I could handle it better than He could. But Philippians 4:6 (NIV) says, "Do not be anxious about anything, but in everything, by prayer and petition, with thanksgiving, present your requests to God."

"Be anxious for nothing." It is a *command,* not a suggestion. Being anxious is worrying; it makes my stomach go into knots and gives me a headache—and a neck and backache. I'm "worried sick." And truthfully, at that moment of worry, I don't even believe that God loves me limitlessly and unconditionally. When I worry, I believe I am alone in this world, that *I have to know* what will happen tomorrow, and that I have to work out my own plan to fix things. A person who worries, at least while they are worrying, is incapable of creative, energetic living. As the Old English definition implies, worry is choking off the Spirit within them, which is love, joy, and peace. It's silenced while we sit and worry.

Exercising *Active* Faith

From the beginning to the end of the Bible, God tells us not to worry. Well, I knew God was in control, but what if His will wasn't mine? Of course I was constantly praying that the surgery would be successful and that the cancer hadn't spread. Yes, I had faith and I knew that, "Everything works together for good for those who believe and are called according to His purpose" (Romans 8:28).

Suddenly, I knew I had to concentrate on God's having had a reason for saving Michael when he was seven years old. I had to believe *actively* that He'd always had a purpose in mind for his life—and that purpose was not fulfilled yet. Michael's accident happened on 7/7/77, when he was seven years old. In the Bible, seven is "God's number of perfection and completion." He was obviously completing a good work in him now. *Could God's purpose be accomplished already? What if He was to take Michael home soon?* I didn't know God's plan, so I had to trust Him and believe in God's goodness, no matter what!

God doesn't tell us merely to: "Be anxious for nothing," but also, "in everything by prayer and supplication [to] make (y)our requests known." His instruction involves an active turning *away* from our problems *toward* Him. I didn't try to *attack* the worry and destroy it. I simply presented it to the Lord, and as I did, He was faithful to give me "the peace that passes all understanding."

"Be still and know that I am God" (Psalm 46:10) was my mandate. I knew I had to acknowledge God actively, to proclaim and believe in my heart—now, when I needed Him most—He is there, He is Sovereign, He reigns. He is Almighty,

All-Knowing, infinitely present. He loves me unconditionally. He'd said He is, "with me always" (Matthew 28:20). *So what am I supposed to do in this situation, Lord?*

I needed to let my requests be made known, and in specific detail. I'd let my mind, with its worrisome negativity, go into every detail of how bad things could be. I should also be able to go into detail on what I wanted and how I was feeling *with* God. I reread the Book of Psalms. The Psalms are a man talking with His God, and most of the time, it seems that its author, David, is a man in trouble. He pours his complaint out, telling God exactly how angry he is and what he wants. In fact, it's OK for all of us to do that. God, our loving Heavenly Father, is big enough to handle it—and He knows what we are thinking, anyway.

In the midst of great trials that trigger the habit of worry, God wants our attitude to remember all He has done for us and to turn our demanding spirit into a thankful one. As we focus our minds and hearts to seek the peace of God, the *shalom* of God will guard our hearts and minds from worry. "Shalom" is a bigger word than our word "peace." It is not necessarily a change in our *circumstances,* but a shift in our *attitude.*

Our idea of peace often implies that everybody *finally does it my way,* or that we negotiate a settlement. The Hebrew understanding of the shalom peace means that in the middle of chaos, I have peace. It means I have peace and harmony in my spirit. It means I have harmony in my mind. I am successful in my thinking. I have prosperity in my emotions. I have love and joy and peace so that my mind and body are both at rest. There is no fear or worry in it.

In his most-famous psalm, Psalm 23 (NIV), David imagines *tomorrow* and what evil may transpire, but he doesn't surrender to it. He says: "Even though I walk through the valley of the shadow of death, I will fear no evil for you are with me." Yes, there is evil in this world, and bad things will happen from time to time, but God is greater! David sees God in all of his tomorrows. And, knowing God, he concludes that, "Surely goodness and mercy will follow me all the days of my life." Seeing God's peace take up residence within you is to see God's goodness in all things.

When God Says "Yes"

The two week waiting period for Michael's pathology report after surgery was excruciating. Though I can't say I didn't still have *some* worry during that time, I can say that it was minimal compared to what it could have been had I not turned to my God and His Word. However, when I got the phone call from my son that the pathology report had come back and they'd "gotten it all," I hung up and broke down completely, sobbing with relief and thankfulness.

One year later, Michael's second daughter was born a preemie, five weeks early, and with a medical problem called "persistent pulmonary hypertension." That sweet little child couldn't breathe on her own, was intubated, and had feeding tubes and needles all over her little body. The doctor said it was *very* serious, and we just had to wait. She said she might get worse before she got better. That was exactly what happened. It was a ten-day ordeal, and I can tell you that there was definitely concern, but little worrying on my part. I immediately went to God and to wonderful people that prayed with me and gave me strength. I guess the more we practice this, the better we get at it!

"If you're going to worry, why pray? If you're going to pray, why worry?" it has been wisely asked. Although . . . I must admit . . . sometimes my prayer is: "Thank you, God, but I really don't need any more of these trials—I've grown enough for one lifetime. I promise You, I won't worry. I'll just be *concerned* and pray!"

CHAPTER THIRTEEN

FORGIVENESS: THE KEY TO PERSONAL FREEDOM

*"Forgiveness is the scent the rose leaves on
the heel that crushes it."*

—Anonymous

It was June of 1991. Michael and Julie Weisser and their children were happy and excited to be moving into their new home in Lincoln, Nebraska. Times were changing for the better, and they were the first Jewish family to take up residence in a neighborhood populated by gentiles. However, not everyone was happy to see them come.

A "welcome package" prepared by the hate-filled Grand Dragon of the local Ku Klux Klan chapter arrived at the doorstep, including a message that said: "The KKK is watching. You'll be sorry you ever moved in," followed by a series of harassing and threatening phone calls. Michael had a big decision to make: move his family out, ignore the threats, get the police involved, or reach out to the Grand Dragon and express love and forgiveness. So, *what did he do?* He began by calling the "KKK Hate Line" repeatedly, leaving messages that expressed the family's love and forgiveness.

"You're going to have to answer to God one day for all this hatred you're expressing toward us, you know," he would say, "and believe me, you don't want to do that." Over time, the Weissers learned that the Grand Dragon, Larry Trapp, was suffering from diabetes, had lost both legs, and had no one to care for him. So Michael asked, "Larry, do you understand that with your disability the Nazis would have made *you* the first to go?" Michael continued to reach out, even shopping for Larry at the local grocery store. Larry was so amazed by the outpouring of love from this man he'd attacked that he not only denounced the KKK but converted to Judaism! In the years ahead, Larry and Michael spoke throughout the United States, sharing their story of love and forgiveness with others. And when Larry was too sick to live alone and there was no one to care for him, Michael and Julie took him into their home. Their children even called him, "Uncle Larry." This man who had been so hurtful and mean-spirited throughout most of his adult life turned full-circle, embracing all he'd persecuted and rejected.

It's a remarkable story of how one hate-filled, hardened heart was changed by goodness, kindness, and forgiveness. How do some people have such an extraordinary capacity for forgiveness? Is it *inborn*, or can it be developed? Do some people lack the basic instincts for anger and revenge, or do just those with strong faith shun these negative emotions? And the Weissers are by no means unique in their display of forgiveness towards a perpetrator of hate. We will hear later of others who unlocked the power of forgiveness, choosing to move beyond anger. But first, let's discover how we can find release from resentment and bitterness ourselves.

The Act of Forgiveness

In previous chapters, we talked about getting control of your mind and emotions and the everyday challenges of relating harmoniously with others and avoiding worry. Another aspect of getting control of the mind, with its automatic, negative thought patterns, is finding a method for dealing with our feelings towards others when their actions injure or defraud us of that which we love.

The method is simple, though the act itself may involve some complex work in the "free will" area of the heart. It concerns a gift you can choose to reach out for, receive, and then extend to others—one that will make your life infinitely more satisfying—the gift of forgiveness!

The Weissers' story of forgiveness is dramatic, almost unbelievable, and involved life-altering choices. But maybe you're facing an issue of anger that is not as dramatic, though still very meaningful to you. Maybe your husband cheated on you, or your wife left you for your best friend. Maybe your sister, whom you took care of growing up, has decided your parents showed favoritism toward you, so now she is bitter and doesn't want to see you again. Perhaps your best friend of twenty years got married, and her husband doesn't want her to have anything to do with you, or one of your children has decided to move out of your life completely. Whatever it is, your personal experience of loss may still be very painful and life-altering for *you*.

> Forgiveness is a decision, not an emotion.

So, what exactly is forgiveness—and how do we do it? By way of a short definition, forgiveness is letting go of the need for revenge and releasing negative thoughts of bitterness and resentment toward a fellow human being. Said one wise philosopher: "If we practice an eye for an eye and a tooth for a tooth, soon the whole world will be blind and toothless."

Forgiveness is about deciding to give up resentment, anger, and the desire to punish, replacing it with a *pardon*. Forgiveness is a *decision, not* an emotion. No one can force you to forgive, and no one can keep you from forgiving. It's a decision to override your own instincts toward revenge and instead trust what Jesus says in the Lord's Prayer: ". . . and forgive us our sins, *as we forgive* those who sin against us" (Luke 11:4). And it's not a one-time event, either. In Matthew 18:21–22, the Apostle Peter says to Jesus, "Lord, how often must I forgive my brother if he wrongs me? As often as seven times?" Jesus answered, "Not seven, I tell you, but seventy-seven-times."

Forgiveness is a process. For some hurtful things done to you, it may be easy to forgive immediately. For deeper offenses, it may take years to experience the full freedom of forgiveness. Forgiveness is *alchemy for the soul*. It transforms coal into gold and brings a magical transformation of the heart. Where you were once burdened, consumed, obsessed, now you are free and willing to move forward. I once heard someone say: "I won't let someone ruin my life by making me hate them." I remember Oprah Winfrey saying once, on her daytime television show, that "persistent bitterness and anger, is like *you* taking poison, hoping *the other person* will die."

> If we practice an eye for an eye and a tooth for a tooth, soon the whole world will be blind and toothless.

Forgiveness is *not* forgetting or pretending that an episode didn't happen. Whatever it was *did* happen, and you want to remember the lesson you learned from it, but without holding the pain ever-present within you. Forgiveness is not excusing the person and what he or she did to you. I remember my Mom saying often, "They don't know any better," whenever I complained about something someone had done to me—and maybe it's true: they didn't. Your living in bitterness is not likely to *teach them* anything now.

On the Cross at Calvary, Jesus said, "Father, forgive them, for they don't know what they are doing" (Luke 23:34) (NIV). Some people certainly *do* know better, but for whatever reason, they may choose to be hurtful and mean-spirited to you. Forgiveness is not giving others permission to continue hurtful behaviors, nor condoning their behavior in the past. And forgiveness doesn't necessarily involve *reconciliation*. The act of forgiveness comes first, freeing you from hurtful, negative feelings. You make a separate decision about whether to reconcile with the person you are forgiving, or not.

Why is it so hard for us to forgive deep-seated hurts? One reason is because you may be filled with self-justified anger. At some point in your life you have been wounded, and you are angry at and hurt by the person who you feel wronged you. You blame the person committing the wrong for how you are feeling. You believe it is their action and not your choice of response that determines your distress. I've been there; I know what you are feeling and thinking: *After all I've done for her . . . given up so much of my life for her—and to be treated like I'm nobody; it's not fair. And she never even asked for my forgiveness. She doesn't care that I'm hurting!*

Thinking back to Ellis' irrational beliefs, perhaps when we are deeply wronged by someone we love, we believe irrationally that certain acts are so awful and so wicked that people who perform these acts should be severely damned. But I hope you are now able to see that you *do* have a choice as to how you react, or temper your first reaction. For most of us, there comes a time when hurt and anger make us feel so sick it impacts our emotional balance and physical health. Yet, for as long as you are unable to forgive, you keep yourself mentally chained to the one who has hurt you. You give them rent-free space in your mind, emotional shackles on your heart, and the right to torment you at all hours of the day or night. But how do we begin the process of obtaining freedom through the gift of forgiveness? Here's my suggested approach.

> To carry a grudge is like being stung to death by one bee.
> —William Walton

Seven Steps to Forgiveness

1. **Recognize who is being hurt by your unforgiveness.** Does the other person burn with your anger, feel the knot in your stomach, experience the constant recycling of your thoughts as you re-experience the events in your mind? Do they stay awake as you do, thinking what you want to do or say to punish them? No, the pain is all *yours*.

2. **Understand that forgiveness does not necessarily mean reconciliation** with the person that upset you, or condoning their action. What you want to find is peace.

3. **Get the right perspective on what happened.** Recognize that your primary distress is coming from the hurt feelings, thoughts, and physical upset you are suffering now, not what offended you two minutes ago or ten years ago. At the moment the hurt happens or returns to your mind, practice some of the stress management techniques learned in Section I.

4. **Acknowledge your part.** Were you honest about your hurt, or did you hide the fact that the behavior hurt you? If you were honest, did the offender accept your feelings as valid? Has it happened many times since, but you keep allowing the behavior? Or did you seek peace by reassuring the perpetrator that it was all right? Did you stay when you *could* or should have left? If so, then you have some responsibility. Make a list of what you gained from the relationship. Did the good outweigh the bad? What were the positives? You don't need the other person to admit they were wrong. Waiting until they admit wrong or ask for forgiveness keeps you stuck in the past. Many of us crucify ourselves between two thieves: resentment and guilt, then we believe that others have done it to us.

5. **Give up expecting things from other people that they do not choose to give you,** no matter how deserving you may be. Recognize you don't have the power to make people behave the way you want them to. You can have hope for love, friendship, and prosperity and work hard for those things, but you will suffer when what you expect doesn't happen. You don't have the power to *make* them happen. Put your energy into looking for another way to get what you want.

6. **Exercise your personal power.** Although someone wants to make you miserable, whether or not you stay miserable is entirely up to you. For those that believe in the power of prayer, know that it *can* take regular, sustained prayer, for a long period of time to forgive profound hurts from a close family member. Your wounded ego or hurt heart may not yield, except through divine grace.

7. **Remember that a life well-lived is the best revenge.** Instead of focusing on your wounded feelings, giving the person who caused pain the power over you, learn to look for the love, beauty, and kindness around you. Tell yourself you don't want to waste your precious life in the discomfort caused by anger or hurt. You are able to forgive yourself, forgive others, forgive life, and even forgive God. Life is filled with beauty and wonder, and you will miss these experiences if you are stuck in remembering the old hurts. You know how it hurts when people don't forgive you. Do you mean to hurt other people by your actions? Of course not. *We judge others by their actions and ourselves by our intentions.* While some are intentionally cruel, most people do the best they can or are simply misguided.

The Hardest Person of All to Forgive

Until now we have been talking about forgiving *others,* but there is another dimension of forgiveness that is the hardest of all: self-forgiveness. Yet it's difficult to learn to forgive others if you can't forgive yourself. *Self-forgiveness* involves accepting yourself as a human being who has faults and who makes mistakes. It means letting go of anger at oneself for past failures and mistakes . . . and then learning from those errors.

> To err is human; to forgive, divine.
> —Alexander Pope

Using the same seven steps above, you can quiet your sense of failure and lighten your burden of guilt.

Why is this final step in forgiveness so important?

When you are unable to forgive yourself, you begin to lose all love for who you are—to reject yourself utterly. This can result in chronic anger outbursts and other destructive behaviors. You can begin to create self-pity, sorrow, and depression as a way of life, as a means of "punishing" yourself. You may become suspicious about others' motives, behaviors, attitudes, and beliefs—even when they are accepting of you—believing yourself unworthy of love, yet furious that others withdraw from your anger.

Forgiveness is the antidote to anger, and self-forgiveness is the antidote to guilt and anger directed at oneself. I hope you will take a moment to let go of the pain and bitterness of unforgiveness and make the decision to go on in your life without them.

Bitter, *or Better?*

It isn't always easy to tell where bitterness ends—or just where forgiveness begins. Lewis Smedes wrote: "You will know that forgiveness has begun when you recall those who hurt you and feel the power to wish them well."

I think of a woman I never knew but who taught me a lot about forgiveness: Gayle Blount, whose daughter Catherine was stabbed to death by a drug addict. After some time, she was able to write to the murderer, eventually visiting him in a California jail. She told him she forgave him and wanted to be his friend. The young man who killed her daughter could not believe the love and forgiveness in this woman's heart! As a result of her "active act of forgiveness," they have been friends ever since.

> You will know that forgiveness has begun when you recall those who hurt you and feel the power to wish them well.
> —Lewis Smedes

Do you think you could befriend and love your child's killer? Gayle said she walked away from the jailhouse that day knowing God had given both of them the gift of forgiveness. *How could this be?* Gayle said she chose to forgive, because she knew that forgiveness brings peace, and with it joy. She wanted the overwhelming joy of knowing that God, according to His promise, would forgive her—just as she'd forgiven another.

After that miraculous meeting, Gayle began traveling from her home near San Francisco to San Quentin State Prison weekly to meet with condemned prisoners, a different one each Friday morning. They talked about prison life, religion, crime, punishment, their personal backgrounds, and their different routes to this caged world behind walls. Her forgiveness impacted hundreds and brought her the peace concerning Catherine's death that she could find by no other means.

You may have read about the Baptist minister in 2000, who was driving in his car with his family when a drunk driver crossed the median and smashed into his station wagon, killing his four sons. Within twenty-four hours this man forgave the drunk driver who'd hit them and then reached out to help this perpetrator of vehicular homicide assuage his guilt. I think many of us would have been so devastated, we wouldn't have been able to even *think* about, let alone *speak* of, forgiveness of the one whose irresponsibility ended the earthly lives of our most beloved family.

One widely reported act of forgiveness was that of Reginald Denny who, after nearly losing his life following the Rodney King trial verdict in Los Angeles, forgave his intentional attackers. Denny was dragged from his truck by rioters and beaten almost to death for no reason. His skull was fractured in ninety-one places; his speech and ability to walk permanently damaged. I remember watching the video of the brutal assault over and over again on television. At the trial, he approached his attackers in a gesture of forgiveness, testifying that he didn't want them to go to jail—and he even *shook one of their hands* on a talk show. What a model of forgiveness this man was to us all!

Holocaust survivor Eva Kor said, after many years of struggling to let go of her bitterness: "Forgiveness is as personal as chemotherapy. I do it for myself." She and her sister, Miriam, were taken to Auschwitz to be used for medical experiments—human guinea pigs. Upon liberation, she lived her life in intense pain and hatred for the doctor who'd performed those horrific experiments on her, and she also nurtured bitterness toward her parents, who could not save or protect her from this nightmare.

In 1993, Eva was invited to lecture before a group of eminent doctors in Boston, Massachusetts, and was asked if she could bring a Nazi doctor along with her, as well. The request startled her, but with some research effort, she located a doctor that had been at Auschwitz and who was overcome with guilt and very willing to go with her. Eva was trying to find a meaningful *thank you* gift for the doctor's willing service when she got the idea to write a "forgiveness letter" to him. She knew it might be a meaningful gift for her, as well, because it would acknowledge the reality that she was not a hopeless, powerless victim anymore, but a victorious survivor.

At first she couldn't imagine *ever* being able to forgive this man, but then she realized *she had the power now*—the power to forgive. It was her right to use it, and no one could take it away from her.

SECTION IV

Getting Control of Your Time

Beyond the "Tyranny of the Urgent"

CHAPTER FOURTEEN

FINDING THE TIME—THE TIME MANAGEMENT MATRIX

"Time is the most valuable thing a person can spend."
—Laertius Diogenes

Time is the fourth piece of life's puzzle. If used wisely, it can make progress possible in the other three: reducing chronic stress and closing the personal fulfillment gap, achieving your personal vision, and living in and enjoying the present. On the other hand, *failure* to get control of your time can lead to increased stress and anxiety, a missed sense of purpose, and increased feelings of inadequacy.

"Google" *time management* and you'll discover there are about 8.3 billion articles, techniques, or references to this one self-improvement subject. *Time management* must be the most ubiquitous file topic on the Internet today. (How could anyone find time to read them all?) Of course, billions relate to the subjects of getting organized, the tyranny of running your life by lists, personal organizers, and how to become more efficient in general.

I'm sure many of you have attended time management classes, or at least read articles on the topic. Yet the phrase "time management" is really a misnomer, because we aren't learning to manage *time* at all; rather, we're learning to more effectively manage *ourselves*. It's been wisely noted that we all have the same amount of time in a day: twenty-four hours. It's what we choose to do within those hours that actually counts.

Asking the Right Questions

So, in light of the important topics discussed so far, how do you manage your time in order to facilitate a personal transformation? How do you align your time with your life plan and what you've defined as your life's purpose? How do you free up sufficient time to address the most important dimensions of your life, those "personal fulfillment gaps" outlined in Section I? How do you spend your best time and energy pursuing your mission, your vision, and the action plans you laid out in Section II? How do you devote enough personal, reflective time to address and change the personal misperceptions that impact your thoughts and emotions, as discussed in Section III?

Have you ever felt like this? It seemed every time I sat down to work on this book there would be a knock at the door or a crisis phone call. Being the "sensitive and available" person I am, I would set aside my work to listen to and comfort a friend . . . or run off to do something for a family member that "couldn't be done by anyone else." After awhile I began to wonder if I was really helping my friend or family member, since I was so preoccupied with the work I felt I was supposed to be doing. By saying *yes* to both important needs, neither was being addressed fully.

Everyone I know believes they don't have enough time to do what needs to be done in a day. In fact, only one out of a hundred people say they have enough time. That one person in a hundred may not have both children and parents to take care of while simultaneously holding down a full-time job. Or maybe he or she does, but just knows how to balance things better than the other ninety-nine of us. The paradox of time is that few people have enough of it, but everyone has *all there is*. How are you doing with *your* time? Please take a moment to write a short answer to each of the following two questions, and then evaluate your use of time.

1. What one thing *could* you do that you aren't doing now, that if you did on a regular basis would make a

tremendous and positive difference in your personal or work life? (We'll return to this later in the chapter.)

2.   If you were to fault yourself in one of the following three areas, which would it be?

a.   Your inability to prioritize.

b.   Your inability to organize around your priorities.

c.   Your lack of discipline to execute your priorities.

Sometimes I would fault myself in all three of these areas! What about you? Some of us prioritize what's on our schedule, while others start with their priorities and schedule them. In my view, it's more important to be *effective* than *efficient*. We could be very efficient at cutting down a tree, only to find out that we cut down the wrong one. So, establishing priorities, then implementing them is the most critical aspect of controlling your time and aligning it with your life plan.

There are many techniques for setting priorities more effectively. One is known by its acronym, POSEC, or: "Prioritize by Organizing, Streamlining, Economizing, and Contributing." This method uses a template that begins by emphasizing an individual's need for emotional and monetary security. It suggests that by attending to one's personal responsibilities first, an individual is then better positioned to take on more collective responsibilities. Here's what the model suggests:

1.   **Prioritize**—your time and define your life by goals (mission/vision).

2.   **Organize**—things you have to accomplish regularly in order to be successful (family, career, and finances, etc.).

3.   **Streamline**—things you may not like to do, but must do (work and chores, etc.).

4. **Economize**—things you should do or may even like to do but are not pressing or urgent (socializing, hobbies, etc.).

5. **Contribute**—by paying attention to the remaining things that make a real difference (family, volunteer/community obligations, and others).

The "A, B, C" Analysis of Time Use

Another approach to time management is borrowed from business: the "A, B, C" analysis. This technique has been successfully used in business for years to break up and categorize large quantities of incoming data or workload into groups. Most of us use it to sort the mail and e-mail that comes into our homes and offices every day. Almost subconsciously we mark items "A, B, or C"—according to perceived priority. "A" items are deemed of highest priority; "C" of lowest. Mail or papers in the "A" folder are the things you need to work on first. The "B" folder holds things you want to save to work on later, and "C" folder items are things you may need in the future but not now. Of course, anything that even looks like a "D" folder item goes straight to the trash can!

The Pareto Analysis

A related concept is called *Pareto Analysis,* the idea that 80 percent of tasks can be completed in 20 percent of the disposable time. The remaining 20 percent of tasks will take up 80 percent of the time. This principle is used to sort tasks into two parts. According to this approach, tasks that fall into the first category are assigned a higher priority.

The "80-20 Rule" can also be applied to increase productivity: it is assumed that 80 percent of the present level of company productivity can be achieved by doing 20 percent of the tasks presently assigned. If productivity is the aim of time management, then these tasks should be prioritized at a higher level. Similarly, I remember how, in my management career at IBM, it always seemed that 20 percent of my employees took 80 percent of my people-management time (usually the less productive performers).

The Eisenhower Method

One of the most useful and popular ways to prioritize is to use the *Eisenhower Method,* a four-quadrant framework developed by U.S. President Dwight D. Eisenhower in the 1950s. It's a time management matrix since popularized by Steven Covey in his book, *First Things First.* It forces us to distinguish between the *urgent* and the truly *important* tasks set before us.

TIME MANAGEMENT MATRIX

	URGENT	NOT URGENT
IMPORTANT	1. NECESSITIES • CRISES • MEDICAL EMERGENCIES • DEADLINE-DRIVEN PROJECTS	2. PERSONAL FULFILLMENT • HEALTH & EXERCISE • RELATIONSHIP BUILDING • PERSONAL GROWTH
NOT IMPORTANT	3. DISTRACTIONS • INTERRUPTIONS • PHONE CALLS • MANY MEETINGS	4. TIME WASTERS • TRIVIAL BUSYWORK • JUNK MAIL • MINDLESS TV SHOWS

SOURCE: DWIGHT D. EISENHOWER, STEPHEN COVEY

Figure 15

As you can see in Figure 15, Time Management Matrix, the top left Quadrant (1) is entitled, "Urgent and Important." The top right quadrant (2) is, "Not Urgent and Important." The bottom left quadrant (3) is labeled, "Urgent and Not

Important," and the bottom right quadrant (4), "Not Urgent and Not Important."

The types of things that would be in the first quadrant are those *necessary elements* and responsibilities we all face. Almost anything that is a crisis, a medical emergency, a pressing problem, a deadline-driven project, or a last-minute preparation for scheduled activities would appear here.

The second quadrant would include activities like: values clarification, preparation and planning for the future, health and exercise, risk/damage management, and relationship building.

The third quadrant might list things like: responding to interruptions, returning phone calls, sorting mail items, reading reports, attending unnecessary meetings, completing "pressing" matters (i.e., bill paying), and attending popular local events.

The fourth quadrant might include our escapist activities, like: watching mindless TV, video game-playing, junk mail perusal (including inane e-mails forwarded to us by friends), trivial busywork, and unfocused time-wasters.

As you break down your own use of time into this matrix, in which quadrant do you think you spend most of your waking hours each day? Many years ago, the first time I was introduced to the model, I actually tracked a week of my time against this matrix and discovered (I am embarrassed to admit it) that in an average day I was spending 25 percent of my time in Quadrant 1 (on the necessities), another 15 percent in Quadrant 2, and over 40 percent in the "Urgent but Unimportant" Quadrant 3—and nearly 20 percent of my time was spent in the wasteful Quadrant 4! Suddenly it was clear to me: Nearly 60 percent of my time was being spent in the lower, less important areas of time use.

Of course, I blamed my job for the amount of time I had to spend "urgently" in Quadrants 1 and 3. That discovery, however, did help me to prioritize my time in accordance with my full life plan.

Both of the "Urgent" quadrants on the left involve forces that "act on us," and both of the "Not Urgent" quadrants are things "we act on," or personally initiate. What I mean is that usually Quadrant 1 and Quadrant 3 activities are imposed on us by others—our boss, our children, our spouse, our neighbors, or our friends. For example, your boss tells you an important report is due a week earlier than he had at first said it was—and the due date is tomorrow; your son "forgot that a major project is due tomorrow," and he hasn't started it yet and needs all types of supplies at the store before he can even begin; and your spouse just called to tell you he forgot he said OK to his sister's invitation to dinner tonight. . . .

By contrast, Quadrant 2 activities are areas that *we* must act on. They *are* very important things, but since they don't appear to be urgent, or aren't imposed on us by others or an urgent deadline, we just don't work on them. We believe we will definitely do these things, but at a more convenient time when we are less busy . . . so, of course, we procrastinate on them. The things we need to do to build relationships and prevent a crisis have to wait while we address—*or catch up from addressing*— "the tyranny of the urgent." What we tend to do are the focused and urgent activities in Quadrants 1 and 3, then the escapist time-wasters in Quadrant 4, perhaps because we are so tired from the *hassles of the day* at work, on the freeway, or in the grocery store. We just want to sit down and watch a few television programs or play randomly on the computer. Quadrant 2 falls by the wayside more of the time than not—until its contents, at last, become "urgent."

In the average person's lifespan of about seventy-five years, an individual spends ten months commuting, three years answering telephones, and three-and-a-half years in meetings.

You may have heard of the man who asked that his tombstone be inscribed: "I've gone to attend another meeting."

The "average person," in his lifetime, will spend thirteen years watching television and three years watching commercials (though less now with TIVO!). I can't find any data as to how much time the average person will spend on the computer in her lifetime, but I'm sure, not counting work-related tasks at the computer, it will be a tremendous and growing number of hours annually.

The "Tyranny of the Urgent"

Why do the *urgent* things always push out the important things you planned to do? It's what one writer referred to as, "The Tyranny of the Urgent." You can't get to the *important* stuff, because addressing the urgent stuff takes all the time you have. What happens is that, at some point, the things that are "not urgent, but important" tend to *become* urgent after a critical event. The guy, for example, that was going to start an exercise program, "just as soon as work slowed down," has a heart attack, leading to a quadruple bypass. *Now* that exercise program becomes "Urgent," not simply "Important," and it gets done daily.

The gal that was going to start eating more nutritiously just as soon as her children got into school full time finds out she has diabetes and high blood pressure. Now her diet and nutritional program becomes "Urgent *and* Important." That report that was so *critical* to get done last night doesn't seem so the next day when you get a call at work that your daughter has been in a serious car accident. Now someone else has to—and will, urgently—present the report. How about all those promises you made to your spouse about spending more quality time together on "date nights?" It didn't happen, and you find out your spouse is having an affair. Is it too late for that "Not Urgent, but Important" activity to become "Urgent and Important?" *Maybe.* Maybe not. Your son's ballgames, that you had every intention of attending but something at work kept getting in the way, are half way into the season, and now he doesn't seem to care whether you attend or not. Is it too late to turn that around?

Right now, if you were to go back over all the tools in this book and work on your mission statement, assessing the seven key areas of your life and developing a list of major life-changing actions, you would probably place them all in Quadrant 2. But maybe if you took the time to make these "*urgent* and important," you could really change your life and realize your destiny. Of course, you are probably asking, "Where am I going to get the time to do all the things in Quadrant 2?"

Start by taking things away from Quadrant 4, and over time, some of the things in Quadrant 3, as well. Start first with watching one less television program a night, or checking your personal e-mail only once or twice-a-day and not reading all of those poems and jokes. Then you can get to Quadrant 3 and start eliminating the interruptions, junk mail, and useless meetings. People often tell me that after being stressed all day at work or at home taking care of children, all they want to do is rest, be mindless, "veg out," and watch TV. Hey, that's OK every now and then. But obviously, if this is a continuing habit, it isn't quality use of your time, and won't lead to lasting fulfillment.

I would venture to say that most people would say that family and friends are the most important things in life, but does this value *show* in your actions and in the way you spend your time? I've never known anyone to say on their death bed that they wish they had spent more time at work. So why is "relationship building" relegated to the hard-to-get-to Quadrant 2?

Remember the question asked at the beginning of this chapter? "*What one thing could you do that you aren't doing now that if you did on a regular basis would make a tremendous and positive difference in your personal or work life?"* Whatever it was, I'll bet it is sitting in Quadrant 2 right now. Was it to begin working out, starting a healthy eating program, or taking care of yourself in some other way? Was it to spend time really *working* at finding a new career direction? Perhaps you wanted to spend more quality time with a family member? Whatever it was, why not disengage from Quadrant 4 and spend the time you save investing in three, four, or five important, life-changing actions before *they* become "urgent, as well as important?"

CHAPTER FIFTEEN

BUILDING A PERSONAL, TIME-BASED ACTION PLAN

"The time for action is now. It's never too late to do something."
—Carl Sandberg

et's take the Time Management Matrix and turn it into a personal action plan. Way back in Chapter Four, "Making the Commitment to Change," I gave some examples of long-term actions we might take toward enriching each of the seven dimensions of life. Remember, these are only my examples, and you will surely think of other, more personal ones for yourself:

1. Family: Engage in a marriage enrichment program to-gether. If you have kids, plan a special family day each month doing something each child desires.

2. Social: Use your newfound time to: _____ (fill in your personal dream activity or hobby); i.e., learn scuba diving and become certified—something you always *dreamed* of doing.

3. Career: Begin to explore other career opportunities or educational development programs to help aid in your advancement.

4. Spiritual: Join a Bible study to help you understand God's desire for your life, and become actively involved in a local church, synagogue, or house of worship.

5. Health: Set up a program with a nutritionist to create the right diet and additional supplements you need. Hire a personal trainer for a couple of months to jump-start the right exercise program for you.

6. Intellectual: Start the application process now to get that degree you have always wanted (Associates, Bachelors, Masters, or Ph.D.).

7. Financial: Enroll in a class or obtain an expert to help you develop a comprehensive family financial plan for balanced investments and a way to become completely debt-free.

Let's start there, and using your personal fulfillment gap (see Figure 11 at end of Section I), fill out Quadrant 2 with three-to-five long-term action items that are truly important to you. These are your *personal fulfillment strategies,* and they should motivate you to find the free time. Consciously strive to maximize Quadrant 2 time. Allocate time in your calendar to carry out these tasks when you are at your best. Doing so can reduce the amount of time taken up by firefighting Quadrant 1 activities, since many Quadrant 1 activities could have been Quadrant 2 items if they had been addressed earlier.

Now go diagonally down to Quadrant 3 and write down two or three opportunities for streamlining or economizing some of the inefficient activities you're involved in, like *meetings*, bill-paying, food-shopping, or *unnecessary interruptions*. Improve your system and strategy for dealing with distractions.

Now go to the right side, Quadrant 4, and write down three big consumers of wasted time to either eliminate or at least *cut in half*. This taps the gold mine that will yield the most abundant supply of time for other things. Seek to eliminate as much as possible of Quadrant 4 activities, either by not spending time on these things or by changing the nature of them to make the time they require more productive. For example, driving or commuting to work can be in Quadrant 4 if the time is unproductive, but there are a number of ways of making this time more productive by listening to tapes and learning new skills enroute. Try carpooling or taking the train so you can work on your mission statement or on setting priorities while you travel. Resign from social organizations that are no longer giving you fulfillment or satisfaction.

In the beginning you probably won't be able to change much from Quadrant 1, but eventually, you will be able to think through ways that help you manage time better, even through these crises and pressing problems, perhaps by using *advanced planning* or *delegation to others.*

PERSONAL TIME-BASED ACTION PLAN

	URGENT	NOT URGENT
IMPORTANT	1. <u>NECESSITIES</u> ADVANCED PLANNING/ DELEGATION OPPORTUNITIES 1. _____ 2. _____ 3. _____	2. <u>PERSONAL FULFILLMENT</u> LONG-TERM STRATEGIES/ACTIONS FOCUSED ON 7 DIMENSIONS 1. _____ 2. _____ 3. _____
NOT IMPORTANT	3. <u>DISTRACTIONS</u> STREAMLINING/ECONOMIZING OPPORTUNITIES 1. _____ 2. _____ 3. _____	4. <u>TIME WASTERS</u> REDUCTION/ELIMINATION TARGETS 1. _____ 2. _____ 3. _____

Figure 16

Procrastination: A Major Barrier to Progress.

If you find yourself putting important tasks off over and over again, you're not alone. Many of us procrastinate to some degree, but some are so chronically affected by procrastination that it stops them from achieving things of which they are fully capable.

The key to controlling and combating this destructive habit is to recognize *when* you procrastinate and *why*, and take active steps towards better outcomes. Most procrastinators work hard—and many hours in the day—but they invest their time more in the *urgent* tasks than the important. They may feel they are doing the right thing by reacting quickly to crisis, and they may be driven by the person whose demands are the loudest. Either way, by doing this they have little or no time left for the *important* tasks in their lives, and neglecting what is important eventually brings about unpleasant outcomes.

Another common cause of procrastination is *feeling overwhelmed by the task.* You may look at a project and simply not know where to begin. Or you may doubt you have the skills or resources you think you need to get the job done. So, you seek comfort in doing tasks you know you're capable of completing. Unfortunately, the important bigger task isn't going to go away because you ignore it; truly *important* tasks never do.

One example in my life was the task of writing this book. As mentioned in the preface, this book emerged from a workshop I created and facilitated for hundreds of attendees throughout the country, across several years. As new concepts were incorporated, it had many different titles, and I adapted it according to the audience I was addressing. After awhile it was pretty easy to differentiate what was needed and customize the material for a group of senior executives, rising stars, teachers, or volunteer workers. But nearly every group I worked with would ask me: "So, where is your book?" They wanted even more information on the topics presented, and they wanted to be able to share what they had learned in my workshop with others.

For years I kept saying I was going to write a book using my workshop and assessments as tools to help people achieve their goals. But I dreamed up every excuse possible to avoid it. The task seemed too overwhelming to me. I would tell myself, "You aren't a writer; you're a speaker, and those two skill sets are very different." I wasn't sure how a workshop could be done through the relatively impersonal medium of a book. I'm an extrovert and get my energy from people around me and their real-time feedback, not sitting at home in my office, typing away by myself. In a workshop, my personality could shine through, whereas in a book there would be nothing but "words on a page" (or so I told myself).

It's true I wasn't a "writer," at least not within the definition of what *I believed* a writer to be, but I did have a story to tell, and it seemed that many workshop attendees, friends, and strangers seemed fascinated by and desperate for information on the topics I knew well, so why not give it a try? Even knowing this was a major goal in my life, I still procrastinated, *big time.* I would get a few chapters done or prepare a book proposal, and then some crisis (Quadrant 1 thing) would come up and derail the whole project. I would stop writing for months at a time. Then, when I would begin again, I would work ten hours straight on a chapter, and then not get back to it for perhaps a couple of weeks. That old adage was true here: "A goal without a deadline is nothing more than a dream."

After making the commitment to finish this book by year's end, I went to a writer's conference and found a publisher I knew would hold me accountable for the work getting done. I developed specific deadlines, saw them as milestones, and gave up other things in my life during this specific time. So, as an admitted procrastinator (at least regarding my book), let me share a little of what I've learned about how to deal with a tendency toward procrastination.

Step 1: Recognize you're procrastinating.

If you are honest with yourself, you know when you're procrastinating. But to be sure you get to them, you first need to *know* your priorities. Putting off an unimportant task is good *prioritization,* not procrastination. Signs that indicate you're procrastinating include:

a. Filling your day with low-priority tasks from your written to-do list. Yes, it feels good to cross off each item you have accomplished, but how do you feel knowing that the big job had not even a dent put in it?

b. Sitting down to start a high-priority task and going almost immediately to get coffee or check your e-mail.

c. Regularly saying yes to unimportant tasks that others ask you to do and filling your time with these, instead of getting on with the important task at hand.

Step 2: Figure out why you are procrastinating.

a. *Why* you procrastinate can depend on both you and the task. You may not be a procrastinator about many things, but just *an important few* (as I was with this book). It's important to understand the reason for procrastination in each case, so you can select the best approach for overcoming your reluctance to approach this task and get going.

b. Common causes of procrastination can be things like fear of failure, fear of success, fear of rejection, poor organizational skills, perfectionism, or waiting for the right mood or right time to begin. Most delays, however, will have to do with finding the task unpleasant or overwhelming.

Step 3: Get over it! Take the Plunge!

If you are putting a key task off because you don't want to do it and can't delegate it to someone else, you need to find ways of motivating yourself to get moving. Some include:

a. Make up your own rewards for work completed by key milestones.

b. Divide big projects up into manageable chunks.

c. Ask someone to check up on you—support partners and peer pressure do work!

d. Identify the unpleasant consequences of *not* doing the task.

e. Shame yourself into getting going, and praise yourself for progress.

"Time Out" on the Ticking Clock of Time

Your life-planning process work finishes on the subject of time, because in my view, time is the most valuable and precious resource each of us has. And proper time use is critical to achieving the personal transformation goals you've identified. For instance, getting control of your life and your mind requires you to get in charge of your daily schedule, to be the master of your time, rather than a slave to it. To truly transform stress into strength, you need to sense that *you* are running your life, rather than life, or external forces, running you.

Changing your life requires you to call "time out" on the treadmill of life *and* the ticking clock each day and evaluate what you're doing, where you are going, what's really important (not urgent), and how you are spending this most perishable of resources. Too often life just sweeps us along as we react to each day's events as stand-alone transactions disconnected from the bigger picture. As we've discussed, however, you have the power to rebalance your life and focus your precious time on what's most valuable and fulfilling to you.

It's simple, really. Reallocate time away from the *least* valuable activities to the *most* valuable ones. When I worked in "corporate America," I used to think that time management was just another business tool to boost personal and company productivity. I have since come to believe that it is actually a key enabler that can unlock the power of personal change. It is not *peripheral* to personal change; it is *pivotal* to it.

CLOSING THE CIRCLE

At the outset of this book, I likened the process of introspection and personal improvement to an unfolding journey—one of exploration, discovery, and enlightenment. Like a long train trip from station to station, the first step often involves the greatest effort as we overcome inertia and get our *big locomotive wheels* rolling forward. For each of us, breaking long-established habits, both mental and physical ones, can be a major challenge. But when we can leave past failure behind and head off in a new direction with determination, new habits can take us to a new destination in life.

Thank you for making this journey with me. I know it hasn't been a vacation, and it has involved the work of introspection, practicing new skills, and discovering your own barriers to transformation. Hopefully the journey has been enjoyable at times, and will ultimately yield the rewards you have envisioned for yourself: purpose, meaning, peace, and fulfillment.

Just for a moment, let's briefly retrace the steps of the journey we have just traveled. It began by acknowledging the daily stress, frustration, and anxiety that many of us face, external symptoms of a more profound set of internal, personal issues. In the first section we began the process of introspection, using the framework of the seven key dimensions of life to pinpoint the sources of *your* stress and determine what's most important to you. We used that framework and several assessment tools to *zero in* on your personal stressors and the personal fulfillment gaps that needed to be closed.

Then, in Section II, "Getting Control of Your Life," we constructed the pyramid of a life plan built on your unique core values, personal mission, and life vision, leading to measurable goals to guide your actions. You began to envision an ideal future state that was personally motivating and that provided a sense of hope and direction. But to achieve that very personalized vision, you needed to first remove the mental roadblocks that constantly derailed your progress and success.

So, in Section III, "Getting Control of Your Mind," we discussed the irrational beliefs that often reside at the depths of each of our brains and cause us to respond to others in illogical ways. We dealt specifically with the challenging issues of emotional control, relationship styles, worry, and forgiveness.

And then, finally, in Section IV, we dealt with the need to reallocate time—away from distractions and escapist activities and towards the more important areas of personal fulfillment you identified, including: relationship-building, personal growth strategies, and the cultivation of good physical health. The ultimate goal is a life of harmony, fulfillment, contentment, and balance.

At the end of this journey you should find a sense of inner congruence as your actions and the time you now spend cultivating your *true,* personal values and life purpose align. It is my sincere hope that you have found this book useful for examining and refocusing your life and that it has motivated you to start your own personal journey onward—transforming a life of stress into one of strength. I'd like to close with one of the most profound and thought-provoking essays I've ever read, one that puts our life journey and destination into perspective.

THE STATION

Robert J. Hastings

Tucked away in our subconscious is an idyllic vision. We see ourselves on a long trip that spans the continent. We are traveling by train. Out the windows we drink in the passing scene of cars on nearby highways, of children waving at a crossing, of cattle grazing on a distant hillside, of smoke pouring from a power plant, of row upon row of corn and wheat, of flatlands and valleys, of mountains and rolling hillsides, of city skylines and village halls.

But uppermost in our minds is the final destination. On a certain day, at a certain hour we will pull into the station. Bands will be playing and flags waving. Once we get there, so many wonderful dreams will come true, and the pieces of our lives will fit together like a completed jigsaw puzzle. How restlessly we pace the aisles, damning the minutes for loitering, waiting, waiting, waiting, for the station.

"When we reach the station, that will be it!" we cry. "When I'm eighteen." "When I buy a new 450 SL Mercedes Benz." "When I put the last kid through college." When I have paid off the mortgage. "When I get a promotion." "When I reach the age of retirement, I shall live 'happily ever after!'"

Sooner or later we must realize there is no one station, no place to arrive at once and for all. The true joy of life is the trip. The station is only a dream. It constantly outdistances us.

"Relish the moment," is a good motto, especially when coupled with Psalm 118:24: "This is the day which the Lord hath made; we will rejoice and be glad in it." It isn't the burdens of today that drive men mad. It is the regrets over yesterday and the fear of tomorrow. Regret and fear are twin thieves who rob us of today.

So, stop pacing the aisles and counting the miles. Instead, climb more mountains, eat more ice cream, go barefoot more often, swim more rivers, watch more sunsets, laugh more, cry less. Life must be lived as we go along. The station will come soon enough.